the
powers of thought

powers of thought

Omraam Mikhaël Aïvanhov

the
powers of thought

Translated from the French

Collection Izvor
No. 224

EDITIONS **PROSVETA**

Prosveta S.A. – B.P. 12 – 83601 Fréjus Cedex (France)

ISBN 2-85566-436-5
édition originale : ISBN 2-85566-378-4

CONTENTS

CONTENTS

The reader will better understand certain aspects of the lectures published in the present volume if he bears in mind that the Master Omraam Mikhaël Aïvanhov's Teaching is exclusively oral.

1

THE REALITY OF SPIRITUAL WORK

I

It is clear for all to see that man is better prepared for work on the material plane than for spiritual work. His five senses, which are the tools he uses in his work in the realm of matter, are far more highly developed than those which give him access to the world of the spirit. And this is why so many of those who set out enthusiastically on the paths of spirituality, often have the impression that they are making no headway, and end by being discouraged.

I have heard so many people say, 'What kind of work is that if it never shows any results ? At least, when you work in the physical world, you can see the results of what you do : things change, something is built up or pulled down. Even intellectual work gives some visible results : you become more knowledgeable, better able to reason or to form an opinion about things.' Yes, all that is perfectly true. If you want to build a house, in only a few weeks you can actually see it there, before

your eyes ; you can touch it. Whereas if you want
to create or build something on the spiritual level,
neither you nor anyone else will see the results.

It is quite possible that, in the face of this, some
of you may begin to have so many doubts that you
are tempted to abandon the attempt to do any
spiritual work and to concentrate, like everybody
else, on activities that give you tangible results. Do
this, if you really want to but, one day, even at the
peak of your career, you will inevitably feel that
something is lacking inwardly. Yes, because your
activity will be out of touch with the only thing that
matters ; you will not have planted the seeds of light,
love, wisdom, power or eternity.

There is one thing that you have to understand
once and for all in respect to spiritual work, and
that is that it involves matter of such extreme sub-
tlety that it cannot be investigated by ordinary
methods. The work we do on the spiritual level is
just as real as that which we do on the physical
plane. When you work on the spiritual plane to edify
something, set in motion forces and waves or bring
light to the minds of human beings, your work is
no less real than when you chop firewood or make
soup on the physical plane. The only reason you
cannot see what you do is that it is a different kind
of matter. Actually though, when someone really
lives on the spiritual plane, he does not need to touch
or see its realities in the same way as he sees those

of the physical world. It is enough for him to sense that they are there. With time, however, they can also materialize on the physical plane.

If you don't know these laws and you keep expecting immediate results from your spiritual work, you may easily become discouraged, and then you may destroy what you had already accomplished, for this very subtle matter is extremely pliant and easy to mould and, depending on whether he is convinced and persevering or not, man's work can be constructive or destructive. Often, in fact, he does a lot of constructive work but never brings anything to completion because he destroys it again almost at once. But inevitably, sooner or later, there will be a physical materialization.

Actually, if you question the Initiates, they will tell you that everything you see on earth is simply the materialization of etheric elements which have reached this degree of physical density. If you have sufficient faith and patience, therefore, all the things you wish for will also be condensed on the physical plane. If you tell me that you have wished for some things for years and that they have still not been translated into physical reality, I shall have to say that that is either because you don't know how to do this work, or because your desires are such that they cannot yet be realized. If your wishes concern the collectivity, mankind as a whole, they will obviously be much more difficult to realize than if they concerned only yourself. While you are praying for peace, how many others are hoping for war ! And, of course, their wishes prevent yours from being realized. But that is no reason to be discouraged. What did Jesus say in the Gospels ? 'Seek first the kingdom of God and His righteousness, and all these things shall be added to you.' The quest for the Kingdom of God brings its own rewards.

Spiritual work and material work are two different things. You must know what to expect and what not to expect from each. From your spiritual work you can expect light, peace, harmony, health and intelligence ; but it will never give you money, glory or the admiration and gratitude of the masses. If that is what you expect from it you will be disappointed : you have got the two worlds mixed up. You must not expect any material advantages from your spiritual work. Your creations on the spiritual plane will remain invisible and intangible for a long time to come.

And now, let's say that the difference between a materialist and a spiritualist[1] is that a spiritualist takes his house with him wherever he goes ! Yes, a spiritualist can never be separated from his treasures, even in death, for they are all within.

1 The word 'spiritualist', in the language of Omraam Mikhaël Aïvanhov, simply means one who looks at things from a spiritual point of view, whose philosophy of life is based on belief in a spiritual reality.

Man's inner achievements are the only things that really belong to him ; they are the only things that are rooted in him and, when the time comes for him to go on to the next world, he takes them with him : all the gems he has amassed (his virtues and qualities) go with him, in his soul and spirit, and his name is inscribed in the Book of Eternal Life.

A spiritualist is rich, therefore, only to the extent that he understands that the only true wealth is spiritual. If he has not grasped this, if his consciousness is not enlightened, he is simply a poor wretch. Whereas a materialist always has some external possessions to fall back on, at least for a time, and this gives him an apparent superiority over the spiritualist. It is up to the spiritualist to understand where his true superiority lies, otherwise he is lost. Ah, yes : 'The Rise and Fall of Spiritualists'... somebody should write a book about it !

The wealth of a spiritualist is extremely subtle and intangible, but if he is conscious of it, he can possess the earth and Heaven too, whereas others can only possess a little bit of the earth. Why is this so difficult to understand ? Some of you will perhaps say, 'But I do understand ! I understand that spiritual possessions are the only kind that we can always be sure of, that nothing material can ever really belong to us because we can't take it with us when we die. But even though I know that I'm making a mistake, I still choose to live a materialistic life, because that's the life I enjoy.' Yes, I am sorry to say that this is often the case : when the intellect understands the advantages of one thing and the heart yearns for another, what is the will to do ? It will obey the heart ; it always tries to satisfy the heart. In order to live that vast, immense, rich life of the spirit you have to love it : it is not enough to understand it intellectually.

My role is to give you explanations and convincing arguments, and I have plenty more of those up my sleeve, but one thing I cannot do, and that is to make you love the spiritual life. To be sure, I can influence you to a certain extent, for, when someone loves something very much, his love is contagious and can influence others ; every human being and even flowers, rocks and animals, even inanimate objects, can communicate an element of what they possess to others. So it is possible for a few rays of my love for the splendour of the divine world to be communicated to you. But it entirely depends on you whether or not you accept that influence.

I always do everything I can to show you the path that it is in your interest to follow, but the desire to follow that path must come from you. When someone loves something, he has the desire to draw closer to it. When you are hungry, you feel that you love food, so you get up and go and look in your cupboards or in the shops for something

to eat. And it is the same in every area. If you love
the spiritual life you will not just stand there with
your arms folded ; you will feel compelled to
manifest your love, you will do everything you can
to satisfy your need for the spiritual life.

To put this in a nutshell, let me say that there
must be a Master to give clear explanations about
what the spiritual life consists of and why it is important to come closer to that life, but it is up to
his disciples to love it and begin to live it. The Master
provides the light and the disciple's heart pronounces its own verdict : to love or not to love, and
the consequences follow automatically. I hope that
this is quite clear ? The light comes from the Master,
the love comes from the disciple, and the movement,
the act, is the result of the combination of the two.
You can picture the Master as a reading lamp : if
a disciple loves reading, he will sit down beside the
lamp and begin to read.

All the wealth of a spiritualist is within him and
in his awareness of that wealth. If he is unaware
of his wealth, he is poorer than any materialist :
materialists always possess something, whereas he
possesses nothing ! But if he learns to expand his
awareness and communicate in thought with all the
most highly evolved souls of the universe, he will
receive their science and their light and joy, and
what materialist could compete with him, then ?
Even diamonds and other precious stones pale

beside the lustre of all those inner treasures, beside
the splendour of a shining soul, a radiant spirit.

A spiritualist who has a vast and enlightened
consciousness is as rich as God Himself, far, far
richer, therefore, than the man of means who
possesses only earthly riches. A materialist does not
know that he is God's heir, he thinks that he is heir
only to his own father, or uncle or grandfather...
and that is not much to boast about ! The
spiritualist knows that he is God's heir and that the
wealth he has inherited is in his spirit. As long as
you have not learned to see things this way you will
be permanently poor and wretched. You will say,
'Heirs of God, indeed ! What fairy-tale is that ?'
It is no fairy-tale. Once your consciousness begins
to be enlightened, you will feel that you are, really
and truly, the Lord's heirs.

When human beings attach more importance to
developing their intellectual faculties, they do so,
unfortunately, to the detriment of other possible
means of exploration and, especially, of realization :
the subtle life of the universe is completely outside
the scope of their investigations and activities. When
they descended into the realm of matter, they forgot
their divine origin ; they no longer remember how
powerful, wise and beautiful they once were. All
they are interested in now is the earth : in exploiting
and plundering it for their own enrichment. But the
day is coming nearer when, instead of perpetually

focusing their attention on the outside world, they will begin to turn back towards the inner dimension. They will lose none of the possibilities they have acquired over hundreds and thousands of years (for their descent into matter will always be a most precious acquisition), but they will no longer concentrate exclusively on the material aspects of the universe ; they will launch into the exploration of other, richer and even more real regions and, in these regions, they will accomplish the work expected of them as sons of God.

Yes, this is something you should know : when a human being dedicates his whole life to the light, his work becomes of decisive importance for the affairs of the world. Wherever he may be and whether he be known or entirely unknown to the rest of the world, he becomes a centre, a focal point of such power that nothing takes place without his participation ; he harmonizes all the forces of the universe in the direction of one luminous goal ; he even has a part in the decisions taken by the spirits on high. Does this astonish you ? There is no reason to be astonished : it is quite normal. Why shouldn't the luminous spirits who watch over the destiny of the world take into account the opinions of other spirits whose radiations and emanations resemble their own ? It would be neither logical nor just if nobody here on earth were allowed a voice in decisions concerning the future of mankind. Henceforth, you must know, first of all, that your voice can be heard when it comes to deciding the destiny of the world and, secondly, how to take part in the decision-making process on high. When you realize this, your life will take on new meaning. You will understand more clearly how important it is to start living a divine life that will earn you the right to make your voice heard in the debates of the sublime entities on high.

You will ask, 'But is a disciple aware that he has this role ?' To begin with, no ; but he can become aware of it. There is always some part of him that participates, that is listened to and taken into consideration, but this occurs in the highest spheres of his consciousness ; his ordinary, everyday awareness does not have access to this level. The physical dimension is so dense and opaque that a great deal of time and effort is necessary before events that occur in the Heavenly spheres are reflected and perceived on earth. To begin with, therefore, in the first few years, his participation will not be fully conscious, but it will still be very real. Otherwise, as I say, it would be unfair if some took all the power into their own hands and the poor spiritualists were not even allowed to vote in their celestial assemblies ! But in order to cast your vote on high, you have to be extremely attentive, conscious, wise and pure ; the situation is not like that on earth, where everyone has the right to vote, even criminals and the insane.

When Jesus said, 'My Heavenly Father is always at work, and I am working with Him' he was expressing this notion : that the Father allows his sons to participate in His decisions. He also said, 'He who believes in me, the works that I do he will do also ; and greater works than these will he do', which shows that Jesus is not the only one who has the right to share in the Father's work. If we fulfil the conditions, therefore, we too can participate. When will Christians decide to understand the celestial truths that would enable them to free themselves and do something truly glorious for the whole world ? Why are they always content to be so insignificant and ineffectual ? Is the ideal Christian one who dips his fingers in holy water, lights a few candles, swallows a few hosts and then goes home to feed the pigs and chickens, get drunk and beat his wife ? It is high time Christians began to have a far broader understanding of Christ's Teaching and to work along the lines he taught them, instead of placidly assuming that they need do nothing more because he has already saved them by shedding his blood for them.

You are on earth as though in a field that has to be tilled and planted. Whatever you do, even if it is only walking in the woods or having a nap, you must always avoid every trace of stagnation ; you must introduce a state of orderly, harmonious activity into yourself, that is, you must work to synchronize all the currents and energies in and around you and make them converge towards the Source of life, towards the light. This is the one and only work required of a disciple. A new light is dawning today in the world which will give new meaning to everything we do, and that new light is a new understanding of the word 'work'.

You ask someone what he is doing and he will tell you, 'I'm working.' But the poor creature is a very long way from knowing what work really means ! No, he may be doing some odd jobs, tinkering at something, even doing hard labour, but that is not truly work. Very few, even amongst Initiates, can say with any truth that they are working. It would be nearer the truth for most people if they said, 'I'm keeping busy', 'I'm making a miserable attempt to work' or 'I'm racking my brains over a problem.' For a person to be able to say, with Jesus, that he is working, he must have already risen to the level of the Divine Spirit in order to learn from Him and model himself on Him. In reality, only God works. And the Lord's servants, the Angels and Archangels, work too, because they have watched and learned how He works. This is why, in the Teaching of the future, the word 'work' will shine with a new light and take on its full, magical significance, for it is by this kind of work that man transforms himself.

Ever since Jesus said, 'My Heavenly Father is

always at work, and I am working with Him', two thousand years ago, no one has ever fathomed the significance of his words. No one has ever wondered what God's work was, how He worked or why Jesus associated himself with His work. The truth is that God's work is immense, gigantic ! Even I lay no claim to have understood it. It makes one's mind spin only to think of it. The work of Christ is a work of the spirit, a work of thought by which everything is purified, harmonized and illuminated ; by which everything is brought to converge on the one Divine Source, so that the waters of that Source may vivify the earth and all its creatures. This is why Jesus also asked his Father to give his disciples life in abundance, for life is the divine water which makes everything grow and flourish. Without that water, that life, man is a desert. Christ's work is to cause life to flow, and it is this work that man, the son of God, must also learn to do.

Before they reach this stage, of course, human beings have to toil through a lot of crude and painful physical labour ; this is the stage at which most human beings find themselves today. It is an essential phase in their development ; until such time as they are capable of accomplishing that other work, they can, at least, do this : they have to do something. Nature has no patience with creatures who do nothing. Every being must be committed, busy ; Nature has no room in her scheme of things for particles that wander about with nothing to do : everything has to be part of a whole, part of a system. Those who drift about aimlessly, without direction or purpose, will be sucked in and swallowed up by other, terrifying vortices. We always have to struggle against the force of inertia, therefore, and learn to work as Christ worked.

In reality, every kind of work can become a spiritual work. For me, everything I do is work. The word 'work' is always in my mind ; I try to make use of everything. I never discard anything : I use it all. Even when I am motionless and apparently idle, I am working with my thoughts, sending life, love and light throughout the universe. Do it and you will see for yourselves ! You will, at last, discover the meaning of your life.

II

According to Initiatic Science, the whole of space is filled with a very subtle matter, a formless quintessence, which also envelops and fills each one of us. And it is up to us, God's children, to give this matter form, to model it as we would model clay and use it to produce wonderful, glorious creations. The Invisible World is not indifferent to what we do with it, It observes our creations and pronounces judgement on them. If It sees men or women who are not contributing to the harmony of the universe, who are destructive, disruptive elements, It deprives them of good conditions and possibilities so that they fall back and revert to a lower level of evolution. And, as you can imagine, between the stones of the earth and God, there are many different levels ! The important thing, therefore, is to know the best kinds of work for the disciples in an Initiatic School : that is what I want to tell you about today.

The first concern of a disciple is to work to perfect himself, to recover the image of himself that he possessed once before, a very long time ago, before he left Paradise, and which he has since lost. This is his principal task : to recapture his original countenance which shone with such light, such splendour and perfection, that all the forces of nature obeyed him. Even the animals were struck with wonder when they saw him. He was a king ; everything obeyed him because of the perfection of his countenance. Later, when he had left Paradise and gone to experience life in the world, he lost that perfection and other creatures no longer recognized him. His visage was no longer so beautiful or expressive, they no longer marvelled when they saw him ; they turned their backs on him and refused to obey him. A disciple, therefore, who remembers this distant past, has only one thought : to recover this lost visage. And, as the visage of man was that of God Himself — for man is made in the image of God — he can find his own lost visage by thinking of the visage of God. By thinking of light, of the splendour and perfection of God who is infinite, almighty and all-loving, even without intending to, man finds his own original image.

If Moses said, in the Book of Genesis, that man was created in the image of God, he certainly never intended these words to remain idle and useless. On the contrary, they were to be an indication for Initiates ; they were meant to show them that they should concern themselves with that image. A disciple, therefore, learns to focus on the perfection of God, on his love, wisdom and power — God has so many qualities and attributes that no one could ever exhaust all that wealth — and, in this way, he models himself and gradually draws closer to perfection. To be sure, it is a very lengthy, an infinitely lengthy task, but it is one of the best : the task of recovering his lost kingship.

Of course, you cannot force human beings ; each one reacts according to his degree of advancement. What can you expect of a cat ? However much you explain things to him, he will only say, 'I can't play the piano, I can't study at the university, I can't command an army, but I can catch mice !' Explain whatever you like to him ; he will listen quietly, purr a little and then disappear in a flash, to pounce on a mouse, and come back, after a few minutes, licking his chops. Each one understands things according to his own level of evolution. And I am talking for those who already sense that there is work to be done in the realm of thought ; they will be delighted to hear about this activity. The others will go off and look for some 'mice', some inferior pleasures.

Of course, I know that very few will accept ideas which are so advanced and unusual ! How many have ever heard of an etheric quintessence that man can model ? But a new age is upon us and human beings must begin to undertake new kinds of work. There are many more that I could describe to you.

Perhaps some of you would prefer something more impersonal[2] than this preoccupation with his own image ? If so, you can think of the world as one immense family whose members all love, understand and smile at each other. Picture a world in which there are no more wars, no more national boundaries, in which all human beings are free to travel and meet others. The whole earth sings a hymn of joy and gratitude to the Creator. Yes, you can think of so many wonderful things for the happiness of mankind ! Isn't it better to do that than to occupy your mind with all kinds of selfish, prosaic things ?

You can also think about the life of all the Heavenly entities : the Angels, Archangels and Divinities, all the Heavenly Hierarchies. Think of their qualities, of the light in which they dwell, of their love and, above all, of their purity ; wish for all that splendour to descend to earth. In this way

---

2 This use of the word 'impersonal' may be misunderstood if it is not placed in the context of Omraam Mikhaël Aïvanhov's teaching concerning the two natures in man, the human and divine, the lower self and the higher Self or, as he terms them, the personality and the individuality. For a fuller treatment of the subject, see *Complete Works*, vol. 11, 'The Key to the Problems of Existence' and *Collection Izvor*, No. 213, 'Man's Two Natures, Human and Divine'.

you will be building bridges and establishing channels of communication so that all the perfection, wealth and beauty of that higher world may really and truly come down to earth, one day.

Yes, instead of allowing your thoughts to roam wherever the fancy takes them, give them some work to do. If you are waiting for a train or in a dentist's waiting room, steer your thoughts upwards and go on with your divine work. What do you think is in most people's minds when they are in buses or trains ? One is thinking of how to revenge himself on someone who has insulted him, another is planning to steal his best friend's wife, a third is plotting to supplant a colleague. To be sure, they all have their minds occupied, but usually with something ugly or vicious : how to satisfy their lusts or settle accounts with their neighbour. You will never find more than one or two who have any communication with Heaven. All the others are lost in their humdrum or frankly criminal preoccupations. I can actually see this. As a matter of fact, it is not difficult to see what is in people's minds, for everything is reflected : nothing is more obvious than thoughts and desires. Human beings imagine that they can conceal them but, in one way or another, they always give themselves away... especially when they most want to hide them !

Oh yes, it is well worth giving up certain preoccupations which cannot do you any good, and

devoting more time to spiritual activities. It is thanks
to such activities that you will, at last, breathe freely
and be reborn. It is they that will free you from the
grip of the Prince of this world, for this domain
does not belong to him. You will have nothing to
do with him ; all the treasures and blessings you
receive will come from other, Heavenly entities, and
you will feel free, free... as free as air !

Try to meditate on these three methods of work.
Yes, for this is essential in our Teaching : how to
work. Everyone can find knowledge and scattered
information in books. There are so many books,
whole libraries full of books, and people read and
read and never do any work. But here, it is the work
that counts. All that I have been saying, so far, is
simply the preliminary theoretical explanation which
is indispensable, no doubt, but it is still not work.
The real work has barely begun ; now is the time
to start. With the three methods I have just explained to you there is work enough for the whole
world for the rest of eternity ; but are you ready
for this work ?

How many, many people I have met who have
told me, 'Ah, the spiritual life is marvellous. I would
love to devote myself to it entirely, but there are
still a few things that I must do for my husband or
wife or children, etc.' Yes, that is all very well, but
ten or twenty years later they have still not managed
to free themselves from all those obligations. In fact,

some of them have died without managing to devote a single minute to their spiritual life ! Why ? Because their reasoning was faulty. You must not wait until you have got everything in your material world organized before beginning your spiritual work, for nothing is ever really perfect ; there is always something that needs attending to, somewhere. Don't put it off : even if nothing is settled, start to live the spiritual life at once, and all the rest will go more smoothly.

Yes, whatever you do in the physical world, nothing is ever settled once and for all. It is like trying to pinch a punctured rubber ball back into shape : every time you get rid of the dent on one side, it appears again on the other side. You think you are going to enjoy peace and quiet at last, because you have retired, your children have all finished school and are married and settled down. Yes, but then they start having their own domestic problems, and you have to help them... Perhaps you have to look after your grandchildren and your house is too small, you are going to have to move ; someone falls ill... and so on and so forth. I tell you : it never ends !

Don't wait, therefore, to begin your spiritual work, the work of thought, for it is thanks to this work that you will find the best solutions for all your problems. Don't count on anything else. As long as you still have not given first place to this work

you will always be subject to disappointment ; you
will never know complete satisfaction or fulfilment.
If you ask Christians about this, they will tell you
that they rely on the Lord, on Providence. But then
why are they always ill, unhappy and impover-
ished ? Why doesn't the Good Lord come and heal
them and make them happy ? Because His hands
are tied ! Yes, His hands are tied and He cannot
help them because they have never planted anything,
or sown any seeds that would give the forces of the
universe a reason to bestir themselves on their
behalf. If they would only sow just one seed, they
would soon see that the sunshine and rain were there
to make it grow !

Yes, sow just one seed — symbolically speaking — and all the powers of Heaven and earth will
be on your side ; you will be able to count on them
to give you results. This is the only thing I believe
in : the work of thought by which you can give
divine direction, a divine meaning, to every activity of your lives and be sure that they are always
beneficial to yourselves and every creature in the
world. It is this work that will help and sustain and
protect you. Most people's professional activities
only affect them very superficially : they go to a factory or an office every day, they work in a labor-
atory or in a political function, they take care of
the sick or teach children, and all that is good, but
none of these things is capable of setting in motion

the powers that the Creator has hidden within them unless, at the same time, they carry on a work of thought that touches the very roots of their being.

Henceforth, learn to do this work, for its fruits are infinite and will be yours for eternity : no one can take them from you because it is something you accomplish inside yourself, where no one else can enter. Even if your job is exceptionally important and interesting, start doing this inner work which will give meaning to all the other things you do on the side. Keep your job, but do this spiritual work as well, for it is the only thing that can really improve you in depth and give a new flavour to all your activities. If you don't do this, little by little, you will lose your appetite for life, and that is the greatest of all misfortunes. This is why I say, in all sincerity, that this is the only thing that counts for me : this work that has to be done day after day and which will, eventually, set the whole universe in motion.

Let me illustrate this : you are standing at the edge of the sea, twirling a stick in the water. Gradually you create a tiny whirlpool and some little straws and a few corks or pieces of paper begin to chase each other round and round. You keep twirling your stick and some little boats are caught up in the movement... you go on and on and, one after another, huge liners start whirling round... and you keep twirling your stick until the whole world is caught up in the movement ! It is simply a question of keeping up the movement. And now for the interpretation of this little story : human beings also swim in an ocean, in the etheric Cosmic Ocean, but they don't know what motions to make in order to influence their environment and obtain results. Well, that is what this work I am talking about is : the motions you have to make to get things moving. Whether you are meditating or praying, eating, walking or washing yourself, you can take advantage of everything you do to become purer, more luminous and intelligent, stronger and fitter. There are so many occasions when you could add just one element to what you are doing, a word or a thought capable of effecting an improvement in and around you. Yes, because, eventually, an inner improvement always produces an external improvement also.

Well, there you are : it is work that counts ; once a disciple has discovered this true work, nothing can hold him back. I remember that, when I was young, Master Peter Deunov would repeat the words : *'Rabota, rabota, rabota. Vrémé, vrémé, vrémé. Vera, vera, vera.'* Work, work, work. Time, time, time. Faith, faith, faith. He never explained why he kept repeating these words, but I thought about it for years, and I discovered that he had condensed a whole philosophy into those three words. Yes, this is what counts : work, but also the faith that you need to undertake and persevere with that work and, above all, time. Yes, for it does take time ! It is no use imagining that it is all going to happen in a flash. I know, now, what *vrémé* is : the years have gone by and I see that *vrémé* is really important !

And work ! How much there is, still, to say about this word ! Human beings work, of course, that is to say they labour to earn their living, but that is not true work. They sow seed, they sweat, they tire themselves out, and they imagine that they are working because they are earning their daily bread. No, they have not begun to work yet, for the word work, to an Initiate, means the great and noble activity of a free being. Spiritual work implies the existence of activities of a particular kind. Today, I have given you an idea of at least three of these activities, but there are many more waiting to be discovered.

2

THINKING THE FUTURE

The future, remote though it may be, holds the promise of a magnificent destiny for the world ; man's evolution is leading him closer and closer to the Godhead. You can have a foretaste of that extraordinary state of beauty, fulfilment and strength, and live in the reality of it in advance, by conjuring up a picture of it in your imagination. This is an extraordinarily effective exercise, capable of transforming your entire life. Unfortunately, human beings have no notion of how to use their minds in this way, and that is why there is so little light or joy and happiness in their lives.

There are two great truths that you must know : the first, that the power of thought is real and, the second, that you can use it to project yourself into the future and experience it in advance. Look what happens when you are waiting, in fear and trembling, to face a difficult situation, to pass an exam or appear in court, for instance : you keep going over it in your mind and worrying about it in advance. And when you are looking forward to holding your sweetheart in your arms, there too, you picture those moments of delight and enjoy them in advance. If you have been invited to dinner or to the theatre, you look forward with assurance to a pleasant evening out with an amusing play or a delicious meal. Well, if your imagination can project you into a future that is just round the corner, why shouldn't it be equally capable of projecting you into the distant future ?

The power of thought is real, both in a negative and a positive sense, and we must learn, therefore, to use it positively. The Initiates have observed simple facts like these and found that they could be extraordinarily effective in helping them to improve their existence. But ordinary human beings never reflect on their day-to-day existence so as to benefit from the opportunities it presents : they drift through life unconsciously, with long faces, always dwelling on what has gone wrong, on all the terrible, catastrophic events they hear about ! There may be no disaster in the offing, but they dwell on the possibility so insistently that it finally happens : they actually bring it upon themselves !

This is something that everybody knows : we live in terror or hopeful anticipation of events before they happen. But why live only in the near future that will be upon us today or tomorrow ? By contrast, the future I am speaking of is the very remote future that will be ours much, much later, in millions of years from now, perhaps. When I see what people think of as the future, it seems so near that, from my point of view, it is already the past. Yes, for what I call the past is men's distress and suffering, all their doubts, torments and anguish. They keep repeating this past because they keep projecting it into the future. By expecting to find suffering in the future, they experience it already, in the present, without realizing that what they think of as the future is already the past.

The past, as I understand it, is a deplorable state of consciousness where there is always something missing, whereas the future is a perfect state of consciousness. All the imperfect states of consciousness that you experience, therefore, all those fears and apprehensions, etc., even if they concern the future, actually belong to the past, for the past is disorder, vice, illness and brutishness. The future, on the contrary, is enhancement, maturation, for we are all on our way to perfection.

As long as you continue to project the imperfections of today onto the days to come, you will continue to reproduce and repeat the old past ; your future will be composed entirely of the bits and pieces of the past that you have projected in advance. It will be a projection, to be sure, but a projection of all that is most vicious and putrid.

Whereas, if you project all that is most beautiful, luminous and perfect, you will live, in advance, in the future that is in store for you. Your future will have already come true, since you are already living in it. When you feel something in the present, it is proof that, even though it may not have materialized on the physical plane yet, it does exist in another form, on the plane of thought, and that is already very important. So, this is what you must learn to do : practise this and you will see that you will be incapable of living as you lived in the past ; it will become impossible.

It is a great blessing for you to receive new truths such as these, every day, for they can make you richer and stronger and enable you to create a future which will be entirely different from your past. This is as true and mathematically certain as the absolute laws of the universe. All you have to do is launch into this spiritual work, and the first step is to keep an eye on your thoughts. Whatever the circumstances, always be sure to glance inward and make sure that you know where your thoughts are and what they are doing. You must be constantly alert, lucid and aware... How often I have asked someone, 'What are you thinking about ?' and they couldn't tell me ; they had never taken the trouble to find out ! It is quite extraordinary : people think all day long and never know what they are thinking ! In these conditions, how can you expect them to learn to control, orientate and concentrate their instinctive energies and put them to good use ? It is absolutely impossible. If you allow any and every force to enter you without your being aware of it or exercising any form of control, it is they that will end by being in command of you. If you want to become their master, you must begin by taking charge of the situation : you must always be aware of what thoughts and feelings pass through you. This is the greatest virtue of a disciple : he is permanently in a state of awareness : at any given moment he knows what kind of currents are moving him and, as soon as a negative thought or feeling enters him, he arrests it and replaces or transforms it.

This is the first work, therefore : to control, direct and master everything that goes on inside you. Take careful note of it, for it is an absolute. True Initiatic Science begins here : never allow any inner event, any psychic phenomenon or emotion to occur without being aware of it. Most people are aware of what goes on inside them only when they are struck down by tragedy and disaster. When this happens, of course, they are aware that something terrible is going on within them. But when the situation is less dramatic, they are not conscious of their inner lives, so they allow all kinds of negative elements to accumulate and, little by little, these things destroy them ; by the time they realize what is happening it is too late to save the situation.

You see, therefore, that your first duty is to be lucid, to keep a watchful eye on what goes on inside you and, as soon as a negative element crops up, to do whatever you can to remedy the situation ; in this way you will become truly powerful. The foundation of all power is in this ability to see what is going on in oneself. And it need not prevent you from being active and working and creating. Some people imagine that if they began to observe and analyse themselves they would never do anything else but, actually, exactly the opposite happens. Self-analysis should become a habit with you. Anyone who imagines that their psychic life is going to organize itself without any analysis or lucidity on their part, are due to be disappointed. It is no use expecting great spiritual achievements if one lacks the most basic qualities even to begin the work.

And the beginning is just that : to be constantly wide awake and vigilant, to recognize the nature of a current of thought or feeling just as soon as it starts moving within you. Sometimes, when you are busy with odd jobs, cleaning something or driving your car, you are concentrating on what you are doing but, at the same time, part of your mind is marinating in negative, vindictive thoughts and feelings. This state of affairs can go on for hours without your even being aware of it ; it is the kind of thing you must become conscious of, for this poisonous underground stream will continue to flow through you until you intervene to change the situation.

You see ? We keep coming back to Jesus' precept : 'Watch and pray'. To watch means to stay awake, yes, but to stay awake on the spiritual level. Your thoughts must be constantly watchful and vigilant so as to recognize and eliminate any impure, harmful currents and elements. Those who fail to be vigilant and watchful are in great danger ; there is nothing worse than to go through life with your eyes closed. Keep your eyes open and be constantly aware of what is going on inside you. Only those who keep their eyes open possess the intelligence of the inner life and refuse to let themselves become the slaves of whatever force or entity tries to enter them. It is so easy to spring a surprise attack on a sleeping man ! So be on your guard !

And what about the other half of that precept : 'Pray' ? What does it mean ? It means that when you have glanced into yourself and seen what is going on, you must intervene and reject one element or introduce another ; in other words, you must take control of the situation and prevent your enemies from invading and plundering you. That is what it means to pray. To pray is to remedy or improve a situation, and the best way to do that is to tune in to Heaven. The human brain is a kind of radio or television set : it tunes in to certain stations, certain wavelengths. If you want to listen to music or a news programme on your transistor radio, you turn a knob and get on to the right wavelength. Well, it is the same thing in your inner life : if you inadvertently turn the knob the wrong way you will tune in to hellish music, noise and conflict. But you only have to turn it again and get onto another wavelength ! By means of thought and imagination, turn your inner dial and tune in to a programme from Heaven. Nothing is easier !

To pray is simply to tune in to the shortest wavelengths and the highest frequencies which put you directly in touch with the Lord ; in this way, you change the movement and vibrations of your inner life. To pray is to set in motion a positive, luminous, divine movement. But this you must never forget : the first step towards freedom and power is to have a good look at what is going on inside you in order to remedy it as far as you are able.

This precept, 'Watch and pray', therefore, is extremely important for the spiritual life. You are obliged to give your physical body the hours of sleep it needs : it is your spirit that must never fall asleep. Sleep soundly at night, but be sure that your spirit keeps on working, even while you are asleep. So many people in the world are unhappy and always in pain and darkness, and it is precisely during the night that an Initiate can help them. His physical body never stirs from his bed, but his spirit travels all over the world, to help and enlighten all these unhappy people. His spirit never sleeps, it is always active. And you can begin to work in this way also, but only if you learn to prepare yourselves before sleeping. Before going to sleep, you should say, 'I am going to leave my body during the night, and go into the invisible world to help other human beings.' Never forget to go to sleep with this magnificent ideal of going to the other world to work for others in all kinds of ways, for it is thanks to this ideal that you build your own future and that of all mankind.

3

PSYCHIC POLLUTION

Everybody thinks ; the only question is how they think. Go and stir up a heap of manure and you will smell a nauseating stench. Well, often enough, that is how people think : they stir up piles of manure and it stinks ! Everybody thinks ; there is not a man alive who does not think, even the idlers who never do anything else, think, but their thought drifts like a leaf blown by the wind. A lot of people think about how to cheat and rob and assassinate others. Day and night men and women use their faculty of thought, but as they don't know how to use it correctly, it does not do them much good. In fact, not only does it not do them much good, but they actually use it to torment and destroy themselves. True thinking implies knowing what to think about and how to do so.

Thought is a force, a power, an instrument given to man by God, so that he, too, may be a creator in the same way that God is a creator : in beauty and perfection. By means of his thought, man can make contact with all kinds of different substances, quintessences and creatures in either the divine or the infernal regions, and if he does not know that thought is creative, he may easily get involved in such negative, disintegrating preoccupations that he destroys himself.

This is why the only thing that is really essential is to be fully conscious and to know whether the way you use your thought and the things you wish and work for, are really and truly good, both for yourself and the rest of mankind or whether, on the contrary, they are detrimental. This is the only thing you should worry about ; there is no need to worry about whether or not your thoughts and feelings will materialize. That is a certainty : sooner or later, good or bad, they will materialize, and if they are bad, it is you who will be their first victim. Unfortunately, human nature is not very highly evolved yet, and the first thing most people think about when certain means and possibilities are revealed to them, is to use them for their own personal, selfish interests, to acquire things for themselves. This is the danger. And it was because of this danger that Initiates in the past chose to keep silence about the powers of thought ; they divulged it only to their disciples when they were sure of their purity and self-dominance. But whether or not these truths about the powers of thought are revealed to human beings, they already use them without realizing it. Whether they know it or not, all men think and imagine, covet and wish for things. Their ignorance, therefore, is no guarantee of safety either for themselves or for others ; this is why it is better to instruct human beings about the means they have in their possession and, at the same time, to warn them of the terrible consequences to themselves if they misuse them.

Everyone should know that nature has given him certain powers thanks to which he is the artisan of his own destiny. He should be told : 'Do whatever you like, but be careful about what you choose to do because it is you who will have to bear the consequences. If you wish for money, worldly success or glory, you must realize, first of all, that you cannot keep things of that kind for long and, also, that they will make you dependent on those who give them to you.' Jesus said, 'The Prince of this world is coming, and he has nothing in me.' This means that 'the Prince of this world' (that is to say, the Devil) possesses riches which he distributes to those who put themselves at his service. Jesus had received nothing from him, so he owed him nothing : he was completely free. This passage from the Gospels is very profound : if you focus all your energies on material acquisitions, you necessarily establish a relationship with the Prince of this world, for they belong to him ; it is he who distributes them. Directly or indirectly, therefore, you ask him for them, you establish a relationship of dependency with him. He may give you what you ask for, but he will demand your liberty, your free will, in exchange ; so be very careful !

Now, there is something else you must know, and that is that the foul thoughts and feelings that human beings spend their time spilling all around them, turn the psychic atmosphere of the earth into a veritable swamp. What is a swamp ? A place that is never purified by a flow of fresh water, so that it swarms with vermin and insects of every kind : they all feed and defecate in the same water ; each one feeds on the filth of all the others. This is a picture of humanity : a swarming mass of worms, tadpoles and frogs in a swamp, all of them busily excreting their own filth and feeding on that of others : disease, hatred, sensuality, viciousness, jealousy and cupidity... They cannot see any of this, of course, but if they were only slightly clairvoyant, they would see the horrible, black, slimy forms disgorged by countless men and women, which accumulate in the layers of the earth's atmosphere.

As a matter of fact, you can sense this when you come back to a town after spending a few months in the mountains. When you are accustomed to the purity of the mountains and the presence of all the bright, luminous entities that dwell in them, you cannot help but sense, as you go down into the plains, the heavy layer of cloud that blankets towns and cities. Even on a clear, bright day, you can see and feel something thick and dark and dense weighing on the atmosphere of a town.

People complain increasingly about pollution, and the scientists who observe what is happening, tell us that everything is polluted : the earth, the water and the air, and that plants, fish and birds, as well as human beings, are dying. They don't know what to do to stop it. And, in any case, even if they did find ways of remedying the situation, it would only improve the external, physical aspect, and that is not enough. For poisonous emanations that are killing human beings are being propagated in the spiritual world as well. If people were truly sensitive, they would realize that the psychic atmosphere of the world today was even less fit to breathe than that of the physical world. People complain of the toxic gasses emitted by car engines, but human beings are doing exactly the same thing : they are poisoning the psychic atmosphere with their toxic emissions : evil thoughts, feelings of hatred, jealousy, anger and sensuality. All the impure thoughts and feelings that cause rot and decay inside men, also produce pestilential, asphyxiating fumes. People blame cars, but what are the cars compared to five billion ignorant human beings who have never learned to master their inner life ?

If there are so many sick people in the world

today, it is not only because of the pollution of air,
water and food. No, if the psychic atmosphere were
not so polluted, human beings would be capable of
neutralizing the external poisons. The problem is
primarily within. When a human being lives in a
state of harmony, his inner forces react and reject
impurities, even physical impurities ; this is how the
physical organism defends itself.

Our vulnerability is, first and foremost, an inner weakness which gradually shows up externally
as well. Take the example of someone who has
tremendous faith and whose blood is very pure : he
can live amongst lepers and people stricken with the
plague or tuberculosis, and never be contaminated.
Whereas the microbes of disease always seem to
catch up with others, even if they flee from them.
Yes, because something is rotting inside them, and
rot is excellent food for microbes ! I have already
explained this to you : pure blood, your pure
thoughts, free you from conditions that are con-
ducive to undesirable entities, even on the physical
plane. Whereas if evil has already penetrated your
feelings, your heart and your desires, the door is
standing open, and it is all too easy for physical
disease to enter and create havoc ! Science knows
nothing about this : it is very behindhand in this
respect. In so many other ways, science is tremendously advanced : it is capable of sending men and
machines to explore the other planets, but it is very

backward when it comes to exploring the inner world. This is why there are no more truly healthy men on the earth. Purity must first be introduced into the inner life, into men's thoughts, feelings, desires, looks, words and gestures. All their emanations must be changed and improved.

How is it possible for anyone to fail to realize that pollution is not only a physical problem ? There are people who are capable of poisoning others simply by their emanations, without so much as touching them. If there were laboratories with sufficiently sophisticated equipment, it would be possible to see that the toxicity of certain fluidic emanations of human beings are so powerful that they can asphyxiate small animals. And one could also see the reverse : that the emanations of a truly spiritual being benefit all creatures, even rocks, plants and animals. The mere presence of a disinterested, loving being affects all those around him beneficially, just as powerfully as the presence of a criminal affects them negatively. Even spirits who have already left the earth, come and find nourishment in his emanations. In fact, if it is still possible to breathe the earth's atmosphere, it is thanks to beings such as this, whose only thought is to spread peace and light all round them.

How can human beings be taught to control their thoughts and desires and to stop polluting nature and the etheric regions ? If they have not even been capable of avoiding the pollution of the physical world, there is even less chance of their avoiding the pollution of the psychic plane, which they cannot even see ; so they just go on releasing their foul thoughts and feelings into the atmosphere and poisoning everyone they come in contact with. Even if the consciousness of those they pollute is not sufficiently developed to recognize the toxic nature of the elements such people emit, that does not prevent them from being polluted, poisoned and destroyed by them. Even if those affected are not aware of it, these elements are active and those who emit them will be punished. Yes, for everything is recorded : how many places you have polluted, how many beings you have soiled and poisoned : all that goes down on record.

Nature is a living organism of which each one of us is a member. Each human being is a cell which has its own place somewhere in that immense cosmic body which sustains, nourishes and vivifies him. If he behaves badly and poisons the atmosphere, he will be a kind of tumour in that cosmic body. And, as Nature has no room for any individual who is a constant source of trouble and infection, she takes a purge and expels him from her body. What do you expect ? Don't you think that Nature is well able to look after herself ? It is important to try to live in harmony with this great universal body which gives us 'room and board' !

And to live in harmony with Nature means to be careful to produce less filth and cause less damage ; to work, on the contrary, to fill the whole of space with pure, luminous, beneficial thoughts. And, as nothing ever remains confined to one spot, as everything constantly moves and spreads in all directions, the waves of purification coming from you will be a blessing for the whole of humanity. But where can we find enlightened beings ready to engage in this work ? There are not many : everyone is too involved in his own interests ; everyone is battling tooth and nail, trying to succeed at all costs. Fists and claws are the weapons they use to make their way in life. And no one has any idea of the tragic cost for mankind of such an attitude !

There must be a network of spiritual focal points over the whole face of the earth, where human beings will be instructed in Initiatic Science and learn to purify the atmosphere ; the inner atmosphere, first of all and, secondly, the external atmosphere ; only then shall we see the coming of the Kingdom of God.

4

THOUGHTS ARE LIVING ENTITIES

I

If there is one thing that is important for you to know, it is that every thought, even the most insignificant, is a living reality. Thoughts can even be seen ; there are people who can see them. Of course, on the physical plane, a thought is invisible and intangible, but it is no less real : in its own region and with its own subtle matter, it is a living, active being. The fact that this is generally unknown is the cause of much misfortune : human beings cannot see or feel that their thoughts are active, that they are either constructive or destructive, so they allow themselves to think whatever they please, without realizing that, in doing so, they are putting obstacles in the way of their own evolution.

God has given the mightiest, most potent form of power that exists to the spirit, and as every one of our thoughts is pregnant with the power of the spirit which brought it into being, that power is constantly at work. Knowing this, each one of you has the possibility of becoming a benefactor of mankind : by projecting your thoughts into the farthest reaches of space, you can send out messages of light to help, comfort, enlighten and heal others. He who undertakes this work knowingly and deliberately, gradually penetrates into the mysterious arcana of divine creation.

If only orthodox science would start to look into this extremely important question of thought ! At the moment, unfortunately, it is only interested in making rockets and bombs ! Actually, I am aware that there is some research going on in the United States and the Soviet Union into the question of telepathy. Take, for example, just one of the American experiments in which two people with telepathic ability were chosen : one of them had to send mental messages which the other one had to pick up. The 'sender' remained in Washington where he was closely guarded by a panel of experts who checked and controlled the whole process. Every message was noted and locked up in a safe so that there could be no possibility of cheating. The 'receiver' was taken on board a submarine which was submerged to a great depth in the Pacific Ocean, thousands of miles from Washington. He, too, was under strict surveillance by a team of experts and, as he picked up each message and wrote it down, it was immediately locked up in a safe. When the messages that had been sent were compared to those received, there was only a very small margin of error.

This experiment proves that the waves emitted by man can travel great distances, although no one knows how far exactly. But then no one knows, either, how far the rays of the sun or of any other star can travel, since the light from a star that is already dead continues to travel through space. And the same is true of human thought : our thoughts are the rays of a sun, the sun that is our spirit. The sun projects a quintessence of prodigious power which his rays — like so many little wagons loaded with food and treasure — carry to great distances in space. And the spirit of man, like the sun, sends out his rays, his thoughts, which carry good or ill with them wherever they go.

Another fact proved by this experiment is that, unlike *alpha*, *beta*, *gamma* and *X* rays, human thought is capable of penetrating great depths of water. Thought, therefore, can produce its effects at great distances and has greater powers of penetration than these physical rays. As soon as you have a thought it goes out from you into the world, where it influences other people's minds. By your thoughts, you are constantly setting in motion all kinds of processes of which you know nothing. What conclusion imposes itself ? The conclusion that if you allow yourselves to entertain negative, dark, destructive thoughts, the laws of affinity cause them to trigger similar thoughts in the minds of thousands and thousands of other human beings. Even if you know nothing about it, this is still the case, and you are responsible and will be punished for it, because no one has the right to influence another human being negatively or to destroy something good in him.

If human beings were sufficiently sensitive, they would see that certain people were surrounded by heavy clouds, by entities of darkness that hover round them and that, after a while, these entities go out into space and do untold damage. And the people concerned have no idea that it is they who are the authors of that damage. Imagine, just for a moment, that you hate someone so much that, every day, you contemplate killing him : even if you don't actually dare to do so, there is still a danger that your murderous thoughts will be put into effect, because another human being, with the same structure and disposition as yourself, may pick up your thoughts through the law of affinity, and commit a crime of which, without knowing it, you are the author. A great many crimes are committed by people who say, 'I don't know what got into me. I had never thought about doing anything like that. I suddenly felt I had to obey the impulse.' They themselves are surprised and dismayed : they cannot understand how they could do such a thing. Well, it is often because, without realizing it, they had been influenced by another. And, of course, this is just as true in the area of feelings as in that of thoughts. Like thought, emotion is a force which emanates from man and travels through space doing either good or evil.

Make up your minds, therefore, to project only thoughts and feelings that will have the most beneficial effects. Whenever you feel that you are no longer in control of the situation, that you are giving way to a negative impulse, you must immediately react and correct your sights. If you are not conscious of what is happening, if you entertain bad, negative thoughts without even being aware of it, those thoughts will go off and do their damage, and it will be your misfortune ! We read in the Gospels, 'Be watchful !' and this means that man must keep a watchful eye on what goes on inside him, not on the outside. You are not in any great danger from things outside you ; it is not always necessary to be keyed up in case someone attacks you in the street.

'Be watchful !' Yes, it is our spirit, our consciousness that must be watchful. This precept concerns the inner life far more than the outer life. Outwardly, most of you are in no danger of having your throats slit, but inwardly, you are liable to be attacked very viciously ! You are liable to be stung and bitten and rended ; you are liable to have boiling water poured over you and be thrown into freezing water... It is Dante's Inferno all over again ! Well, all these torments are the remnants of thoughts that took their source in you and are now coming home to roost. It is essential for you to know and understand, henceforth, that nothing is more important than to be aware and vigilant about your thoughts. Obviously, this is not something that you can learn to do overnight. For some time to come you will still be subject to certain tribulations but, one day, you will be in a position to master the situation.

II

Depending on their strength, nature and quality and on the intention and emotion with which they are charged, man's thoughts seek out specific beings or objects. Some thoughts have a very short life, whereas others can survive for hundreds and even thousands of years. Yes, there are still thoughts abroad in the world today, that have been there since the days of Ancient Egypt, Syria or Chaldaea or even Atlantis. Some of these thoughts are so evil and venomous that they are still destructive whereas others, on the contrary, are still the source of great blessings.

Each thought is like a human being, it tries to live as long as it can and, when it has no more strength left, it dies. And all thoughts of the same nature get together and reinforce and amplify each other. But we are not in the habit of thinking of thoughts as living entities ; there is no mention of this in the official science we are taught ; it is something that is completely unknown. Only Initiatic Science has studied this question, and it teaches not only that thoughts are living entities, but that they are not actually created by man. They can enter and dwell in man, to help or hinder him, but he does not create them himself : he creates only the conditions they need to come and visit him. The process is exactly the same as for children : a man and woman do not create their child, that is to say, his spirit ; they only build his 'house', the physical body in which his spirit dwells. And the 'house' they build may be a shack or a palace, depending on the materials they have managed to procure.

So, man does not create his own thoughts ; he simply attracts some and repulses others, for the laws of attraction and repulsion apply in this domain, as in so many others. If man created his own thoughts, he would be able to get rid of them as easily as he brought them into being but, as you know from personal experience, that is not the case. How often a swarm of thoughts have attacked you, like a cloud of angry wasps or mosquitoes, and you have been unable to drive them away ! Why ? Because you have created the conditions that attract them ; the impurities that you have allowed to accumulate in yourself attracts creatures that like that kind of dirt. But if you purify yourself, you will soon see what kind of thoughts come to you. Thoughts exist in every region and on every level of space, all the way to the world of Ideas of which

Plato spoke. What are Ideas ? They are the eternal Principles, the Archetypes, the Powers that are constantly at work forming and fashioning the universe. They are divinities. Each Idea is a divinity.

You will ask, 'But what is it in us that attracts ideas ? How do we set about it ? Do we create certain ideas which then attract others ?' No, the truth is that when we come into this world we are already equipped with a certain number of ideas, and these ideas are like workers who collaborate in the construction of our existence.

And each one of us, also, is a thought. The entire universe is peopled with God's thoughts ; God thinks, and the visible and invisible creatures that exist are all His thoughts. You could say, in fact, that only God thinks and that we think only to the extent to which we are capable of approaching God and identifying with His Spirit. As long as we are not filled with the Divine Spirit, we are available for other beings to use us and think through us.

To be sure, those other beings can be of various kinds. When you are in a state of extraordinary joy and delight, for instance, when you are filled with awe and wonder and have very exalted, very pure thoughts, you can be sure that these thoughts are powerful spirits that have come to reward you and help you to continue in the right direction. Their presence creates an exalted state of mind in you, and then, when they leave you again, you lose that state of mind and, however hard you try, you cannot recapture the thoughts that created it. If those thoughts had been your own creations, you would be able to get them back as and when you pleased, as often as you pleased. But they are not, they are simply your guests ; they have their own itinerary to follow, their own programme, and when you prepare suitable conditions for them, they visit you briefly to give you their blessing and then go on their way.

But, as I said a few moments ago, thoughts are also entities that are at man's service, and thanks to which he can attract other entities. Imagine, for instance, that you have a household of servants and that you tell them to prepare a banquet and invite a certain number of guests. Well, your guests are not you, and your servants are not you, either. You are the master or mistress of the household ; they are your servants. Similarly, from the time of his birth, man has a certain number of servants at his beck and call : not only his thoughts, but also his feelings and impulses which are also independent entities. I am well aware that it is very difficult for you to accept such a notion, because it is so different from everything you have ever learned. In fact, there are scientists who claim that thoughts are simply a secretion of the brain, just as bile is a secretion of the liver ! No, this is completely false.

As long as we have these servants within us,

therefore, we continue to have the possibility of preparing the proper conditions for Heaven to come and dwell in us in the form of talents, virtues and powers. And when we cease to be guided by reason, these entities leave us, for they cannot bear to live in such conditions : they cannot bear the absence of beauty, the revolting stench, the rot, so they go away. If we created our own thoughts, we should be able to manufacture new gifts and talents for ourselves or, at least, hold on to those we have and not let them slip from us. But how many singers, painters and musicians — even healers and clair-voyants — continually lose their talents !

Invisible entities are constantly entering or leaving us. There is a great deal of movement going on within us, for each human being is like a house of several storeys with countless rooms on each floor and a constant coming and going of tenants. Yes, and as often as not, the wretched landlord has been locked up in a little cell in some remote corner of the house, and nobody obeys him or listens to what he has to say. His tenants and servants have taken over and imposed their will on him. They have fomented a revolution, shut him up in his cell and condemned him to live on just enough bread and water to keep body and soul together, and it is they who are in command !

Don't you believe me ? I assure you, there are a great many people who are no longer masters in their own house, no longer rulers of their own kingdom. All those who live within them eat and drink and enjoy themselves at their expense, and there is nothing they can do about it : nobody listens to them. Why ? Because they have not lived reasonably : they have abandoned themselves to their basest appetites and whims and, in this way, attracted more and more inferior entities until, one day, they found themselves tied hand and foot. The only thing they can do now is take stock of the situation ; they are quite incapable of changing it. To change it, they are going to have to look for some friends and allies capable of helping them to drive out their enemies and take control of their kingdom once again. That is their only hope ! And they must not put it off : if they don't react very rapidly the situation will go from bad to worse.

Of course, I know that it is difficult for you to understand that it is not you who create your thoughts, and yet that is the truth. Man disposes of quantities of thoughts which are his servants, just as a father may have dozens of children who live with him and help him in his work, but it was not he who created them. The father and mother provide the physical body, but the spirit of the children comes from somewhere else. And insofar as we are spirits, each one of us, also, is a thought ; but it was not we who created that thought, it was the Lord. Each one of us, therefore, is a powerful, well-armed thought which has a great many other thoughts at its service.

We are a creation of God ; it is God and God alone who creates thoughts and sends them into the world. The Angels and Archangels are also thoughts created by God, and the universe is the Temple which God has peopled with His thoughts, that is to say, with servants, entities, spirits. The Lord created thoughts, spirits ; and the universe was fashioned to be their dwelling place.

In the same way, man prepares suitable conditions, a dwelling place, for the thoughts that come to him. He does not create his thoughts any more than he creates the life that he transmits to his children. Parents are tutors and guardians, their children have been sent to them to be brought up and educated ; they don't even know where they came from nor who they are. What they must know, however, is that, one day, they will have to give an account of how they have carried out the task entrusted to them. If they have been negligent and inattentive they will be punished ; but if they have been faithful guardians they will be rewarded for the work they have done.

Think about this comparison between our thoughts and our children. It may seem rather simplistic, not philosophical enough, and yet it is the truth. You are surrounded by your thoughts as though by your own children. Yes, a whole brood of little ones ! And you have to feed and wash and educate them. Without your realizing it, some of them have battened on to you and are draining you of all your strength ; others rampage round the world, stealing and plundering. But the invisible world has its own kind of police force, and they will hold you responsible for the damage caused by your children ; when this happens you will be brought before the courts on high and ordered to pay damages and costs ! Is your life full of trials and tribulations, bitterness and distress ? And do you still wonder why ? The answer is, simply, that you still have debts to pay in the invisible world.

This is why I have always insisted on the importance of using your thoughts and desires to form angelic, divine children, who will always be with you and bring only blessings on you.

5

HOW THOUGHT MATERIALIZES ON THE PHYSICAL PLANE

It is necessary to keep coming back to this question of thought : what it is, how it works, how it materializes physically and what conditions must be present for it to materialize. A great many things in our lives depend on a proper understanding of this question. If it is not clear in your minds, you will always have a certain number of problems that you are unable to solve.

Some spiritualists read books which tell them that the power of thought is unlimited and, without studying the question any further to find out when that is the case and when it is not, launch enthusiastically into exercises of mental concentration, in the expectation of getting results on the physical plane. And then, of course, as they don't get them, they are very disappointed. Yes, well they could go on concentrating for years, but they would still not get the results they hope for, because they have not studied the question properly. Thought is all-powerful, that is true, but in order to understand what the power of thought consists of, you have to know in what region it works, what materials it uses and how its influence filters down from one level to another until it reaches the physical plane.

Nature has established certain laws. Why do men waste so much time and effort in the attempt to thwart those laws ? If you want to get a lump of sugar to jump out of the sugar bowl into your mouth, you can concentrate for all you are worth, but it won't happen, and you will be discouraged and disappointed. Whereas, all you have to do is stretch out your hand, pick up a lump of sugar and pop it into your mouth : no fuss or bother ! Nature gave you a hand which you can use to pick things up. You will say, 'But what can one do with thought, then ?' With thought you can do far more important things than that, but you must know its nature and its mechanism ; you must know how it works.

Thought is a force, an energy, but it is also an extremely subtle matter which operates in a remote region, far removed from the physical plane. Take the example of an antenna : you have all seen different kinds of radio or television antennae on the roof of a house or the top of a tower, and you know that they are used to pick up waves, vibrations. From the day they were put up they have been constantly receiving something from the atmosphere : do you think that they have accumulated some par-

ticles of what they have picked up from the air ?
Are they any bigger or heavier now than they were
in the beginning ? No, their weight and volume are
still the same : they have been receiving something,
but that something is not material. There always has
to be a physical, material point of departure to produce waves, but the waves themselves are not
material. Antennae pick up vibrations, certain
wavelengths, therefore, which they then transmit to
various instruments, and these instruments, in turn,
transmit them to others, thereby triggering a
physical reaction.

Or take the example of a ball : suppose I kick
or hit a ball with a bat, I am communicating energy
to it. I am not adding anything material to the ball,
but it is set in motion by the energy I have transmit-
ted to it and it will continue to fly through the air
or roll along the ground until that energy has all
been used up or an obstacle gets in its way.

These examples may help you to understand that
the thoughts we formulate do not touch the visible,
dense layers of matter ; they can only touch and
transmit vibrations to the kind of matter that comes
closest to their own, to the subtlest elements that
exist in ourselves and others. Thought communicates itself, therefore, in exactly the same way
as kinetic energy communicates itself to a ball.

Thought as energy, force or vibration is picked
up by the antennae connected to certain centres in

our bodies. When these antennae, which are located in the brain or on an even higher level, in the etheric region, start to vibrate, they transmit messages to other instruments and various effects are set in motion, recordings are made, energies and forces circulate. None of this is visible, of course ; it would be useless to try to see the effects on the physical plane. But something has happened on the subtle plane and, if you do what needs to be done to pass on this communication to other, less subtle regions and less refined instruments, you can completely restore the whole system of contacts and communications. A human being is like a factory, fully equipped with machines and instruments of all kinds ; all the tubing and cables are in place ; the only thing that remains to set it all in motion is to push one little button that is connected to a series of gears and transmission belts ; as soon as you push it, all the machines start functioning.

If a human being succeeds in setting up an analogous series of connections within himself, his thought can produce tangible results on the physical plane immediately. But if the channels of communication are not properly connected from one level to another, the effects of thought cannot be immediate : there will be gaps, dead zones where the current is not getting through.

The thoughts projected by man produce an effect in his highest regions, therefore, and set his subtlest instruments in motion, but they cannot produce physical effects until the lines of communication are open. As soon as communication has been established, the energies are free to circulate and produce material results. And, when this is the case, thought is truly powerful, truly magic and capable of manifesting itself in all its fullness.

Now, let's try to make this completely clear, for it is absolutely true that thought can be materialized, but you have to understand how it happens. Take the example of a man who becomes a thief. At the beginning of his career, he goes no further than the simple thought : 'Aha, there's no one about ; I could easily slip in and take that...' He still has no real desire to do so and, besides, he doesn't have the courage ! But he continues to think about it from time to time and pictures the scene in his mind : he sees the crowds in the streets or buses and imagines himself slipping his hand into someone's pocket or purse or snatching something from a shop counter. All this is on the mental level ; he is still incapable of actually doing anything. But the thing is that, as his thoughts are all being recorded, they set certain wheels in motion on the astral plane and, from there, they can quite easily move down onto the level of matter. And, for our fledgling thief, the realization of his thought on the level of matter means the gesture, the concrete application, the actual theft. To begin with, it was as though nothing was happening at all ; nothing could be seen of what this man was plotting : outwardly he seemed perfectly honest. But his thoughts had already reached the level of feeling ; he had already begun to wish with all his might for their realization, and from there to the material gesture is only a short step. The lines of communication are in place, the connections are already being made and, one fine day, his hand simply reaches out, as though it were the most natural thing in the world, and takes somebody's wallet or a valuable object. You can see that his thought, which began by being high up on the mental plane, descended onto the astral plane, the plane of desire, and, from there, onto the physical plane. How can you continue to believe that thought does not produce material results ?

Take another example : that of a very gentle, idealistic, peace-loving man who is so mild that when someone strikes him, he turns the other cheek ! But then, one day, he starts reading historical books and begins to be fascinated by certain thinkers or statesmen who revolutionized society and led the masses into all kinds of adventures. He becomes so absorbed in the story of their lives, continually nourishing his passion on their writings, that he gradually becomes very bold and adventurous himself. Finally, he becomes a political activist, discovers that he is capable of swaying a crowd and ends by leading a revolution in his country. The whole adventure began as ideas and theories, nothing but a philosophy. How can you deny that thought is extraordinarily powerful ? It is invisible, it cannot move a lump of sugar, but it can move millions of men !

Thought can pass through walls and physical objects without a trace ; in order to get it to take effect on the material level, you have to build bridges, that is to say, a series of intermediaries. Send it through these intermediaries and you will see that it is capable of shaking the universe to its foundations. This is the meaning of that famous saying of Archimedes : 'Give me a lever and I will move the earth !' The lever is an intermediary and an intermediary is always necessary. Thought is powerful and effective on condition that the intermediaries are there to allow it to descend all the way to the level of matter.

You all have wonderful, divine ideas, I know ; but what results have they produced ? None ? That proves that you still have some work to do to bring your ideas down onto the physical plane. Yes, that is the important thing : to get them to descend into matter. You say, 'I have an idea !' Well done ! Good for you ! But your idea will leave you to die of hunger and thirst if you don't know how to materialize it by your actions. It is not enough to have ideas. A great many people have ideas, but they live in such a way that there is never any connection between their ideas and their actions. There must be an intermediary, a bridge, and that intermediary is feeling, emotion. When it enters the dimension of the emotions, an idea takes on flesh and blood and becomes capable of influencing matter.

Feeling, therefore, is the lever that is capable of touching matter. Thought is too remote, too subtle ; it passes matter by without touching it or causing it to vibrate. It can only touch our 'antennae', the subtlest of our instruments which exist on a very high level in the domain of the spirit. In order to reach the level of matter, the spirit has to pass through the soul, that is to say : through the mind and the heart. Let me explain this to you by analogy, with the help of a phenomenon familiar to all of you : the action of the sun on air, water and earth.

The sun heats the air and water vapour contained in the atmosphere and, when the air is warm, it tends to rise, thereby creating zones of low pressure, whereas the colder air is compressed as it is forced down to the ground, thus creating zones of high pressure. The air moving from the zones of high pressure towards the zones of low pressure forms the wind and, when the difference in pressure becomes very great, the winds become stronger and more violent, sometimes producing devastating tornadoes and hurricanes. But that is not all : the sun also heats the water of oceans, seas, lakes and rivers, and turns it into water vapour which rises into the air. When the air reaches the point of saturation, the water vapour is transformed into rain or snow and then showers and storms act on the earth, creating the contours of hills and valleys. Day after day, these atmospheric phenomena occur over the whole surface of the earth, and it is the sun that causes them.

In man, the sun corresponds to the spirit, the air to thought, the water to feelings and the earth to the physical body. When the spirit acts on thought, thought, in turn, acts on the feelings, and the feelings surge into the physical body, causing it to move, to make a gesture, to speak. The physical body, therefore, is moved by feeling, feeling is aroused by thought and thought is born through the influence of the spirit. This mechanism is there, before our eyes, every day : under the influence of air, water acts to model the earth, to sculpture it and give it form. Hollow areas are filled with alluvial deposits, hillsides and cliffs erode and slide into the sea, and so on. In the same way, man can act on his own physical body, on condition that he uses air and water as his intermediaries. And, in this case, air represents the nervous system and water represents the blood. The nervous system regulates the circulation of the blood in our bodies, and the blood deposits certain elements and washes away others, thus modelling the physical body.

It is possible to study this question in much greater detail but, for the time being, I simply wanted to sketch out some of the main points for you. It is the general idea that interests me, and from that idea we can draw the following conclusion : if human beings knew how to interpret and apply to their inner lives, this normal, natural process of the sun's action on the earth through the intermediary of air and water, they would be capable of tremendous transformations, both inwardly and outwardly. This is what the power of thought consists of !

The most important thing to realize, therefore, is that thought cannot exert its influence directly on the physical plane : it needs intermediaries. We don't pick up burning coals or help ourselves to soup with our hands ; we use tongs or a ladle. And the pattern is the same in every domain. Do you want to know what an arm is, for instance ? An arm is the intermediary between a thought and an object. When I pick up a lump of sugar, who is actually performing the action ? My thought. Yes, through the arm that serves as its intermediary, it is my thought that is acting. And suppose my thought remains inactive ; what then ? I still have an arm, but if there is no thought and no desire to stimulate it to take a lump of sugar, it will not do so. It is in this sense that one can speak of the power of thought.

It is always thought that urges men forward or holds them back, it is thought that gives rise equally to war and devastation or to the noblest endeavours. Yes, thought is active, but it needs an arm in order to materialize concretely. And man is also an executor, an arm. Man's arm is a symbol of the whole man, and man himself is the symbol of another kind of arm. Your arm represents you ; you represent an arm for your thought, and your thought can be an arm for yet other thoughts which exist on a much higher plane, and so on, all the way to the Deity, who uses all the arms of the universe, that is to say : all creatures.

You can see, now, why Initiatic Science has always taught that all the things we see in nature : animals, insects, trees, mountains, lakes, fruit and flowers... all these things are crystallized thoughts. Yes, everything is a thought that was originally projected by God and has become visible. You too : you are all thoughts that have materialized. Man is a thought, an idea. In fact, if you want to know what kind of thought or idea gave rise to a particular creature, it is sufficient to see the form that it has taken. If a man is perfect, it means that the thought that gave birth to him was perfect. Every thought materializes : an octopus, a worm, a scorpion and a tiger have all taken on the colour, shape and general appearance of the thought that dwells in them : a thought of cruelty, wickedness, hatred, deceit or sensuality. Every thought, therefore, every idea (although the words, 'idea' and 'thought' mean two different things) has its own form, colour and dimension. This is why the Initiates see and envisage the world as a creation, a condensation of thought, of divine thought.

When a man has divine thoughts and desires they assume immediate reality somewhere in the universe, and also in the man himself. And when men are evil, vindictive and cruel, their thoughts and desires also become a reality, in some form or another, somewhere in the world, as well as in themselves. This cannot be seen at once, of course, but, sooner or later, everything will be seen. Another thing you must know, is that poisonous plants and vicious animals are fed, sustained and nourished by the evil thoughts and feelings of human beings. Yes, the venom distilled by human beings goes to reinforce the malignity of these animals and plants. Whereas the good thoughts and feelings of all visible and invisible creatures, go to reinforce all that gives beauty, charm and fragrance to nature. Without knowing it, therefore, we participate in both the best and the worst of creation.

The thing that prevents human beings from understanding the effects of their thoughts and feelings is the fact that these effects are not immediately apparent. But you should not need immediate effects in order to be convinced. People say, 'We can't see any of that ; it is impossible to believe it !' Initiates, on the other hand, have taken the time and trouble to observe, examine and verify what happens in nature, and they know that everything ends by coagulating, condensing. The crystallization of salts is an illustration of what happens throughout nature. You look at a liquid solution in which a chemist has dissolved some salts. 'The liquid is perfectly clear', you say ; 'It's pure water.' But the chemist says, 'Wait ; let's heat it.' and, under the influence of heat, the crystals begin to form. If you give salts the proper conditions they will crystallize. And man has a great many things in his head : you only have to give them the right conditions and you will see them materializing in acts.

But now I must tell you that thought can also be materialized in another way. Suppose somebody wants to put some salt in his soup by the power of thought alone : well, as I have already said, it is much better to use your hand to put salt in your soup ! But if someone knows the laws of materialization of thought as they are practised in spiritualistic seances, he will be able to materialize a fluidic hand and, with that hand, which is condensed but still invisible, he will pick up the salt and sprinkle it into his soup. Thought, therefore, is capable of touching matter, but to do so it needs the intermediary of another plane ; it has to be enveloped in etheric matter, which is denser than thought, and this etheric matter makes direct contact with physical matter, for they both belong to the same region and have much in common.

If we want thought to act on objects and other beings, we must condense it. This is always possible : when a man works for a very long time on his mental creations and even gives them some particles of his own matter, he ends by clothing his thought-forms in physical matter. There are fakirs who can do this very rapidly, because they know techniques that enable them to materialize a thought-form and make it visible and tangible. But what you can obtain by these methods will not be of a very exalted nature. To produce a cloud of dust by the power of thought, or even to materialize fruit and flowers is, of course, fantastic, but what use are such exploits for the establishment of the Kingdom of God ?

You must understand that Initiates are not at all interested in producing phenomena of this kind. They could do so if they wanted to, of course, but their Science has taught them a great many other things and led them to understand that activities of this kind are uneconomical ; they would only cause them to waste a great deal of time and energy for no useful purpose. It is so much easier to use your hand to put salt in your soup !

But then, what do Initiates spend their time on ? On other activities which are far more important.

They spend their time working to produce beneficial transformations in men's heads. For, once these transformations have taken place in men's heads, their heads will find ways of communicating with their feelings, and their feelings with their acts and, in this way, human beings will, eventually, move in the right direction. Isn't this a much more useful activity than to concentrate on moving, lifting or bending heavy objects ? For when you spend your time and energy on activities of that kind, you are not doing anything in the hearts, souls or minds of men in order to improve and instruct them and bring them closer to God. Some yogis and magicians concentrate on trivial, unimportant phenomena of this kind, whereas true Sages will say : 'All that is possible, to be sure. We can do it, too, but what would be the point ? We would only be wasting a lot of time and energy and what would we gain ? So little ! No, it is simply not worth it. We prefer to spend all our energy on another kind of work which is millions of times more important for the future of mankind.' Yes, that is the reasoning of the wise.

I am truly astonished when I see certain fakirs or yogis who have taken the trouble to perfect the most unlikely exploits just for the benefit of sightseers. Anyone who has exceptional psychic capacities and powers of thought or great powers of concentration, should use them to seek the com-

ing of the Kingdom of God, not as an entertain-
ment in a circus !

As far as you are concerned, therefore, I don't
advise you to start trying to practise magic. When
we possess this knowledge we must use it exclusively
for a worthwhile task of supreme importance for
the future of humanity. And, since you now know
that, sooner or later, all thought eventually becomes
physical reality, you must grow in hope and courage
and not be so anxious to see immediate results. If
you count too much on obtaining results immediately, you will only be disappointed and discouraged,
and then you will abandon your efforts... and that
would be a great pity.

So, what are we doing here, in the Universal
White Brotherhood ? We are working to build
bridges. Yes, I have said it before : you are all
bridge-builders ; you are building bridges between
yourselves and the sun, between your thought and
matter and, as bridge-building is a delicate and com-
plicated business, it takes a very long time. But once
the whole system is in place, you will see that
everything works beautifully ! You will only have
to push one button and the whole factory will start
to hum as the machines begin to function... on condition, of course, that they are all plugged in to the
mains !

Look at a watch, for example : when you wind up the spring it sets in motion a complex system of wheels and gears in which each one transmits movement to the next one and, finally, to the hands which tell you what time it is. The spring is not directly connected to the hands ; the movement would be too sudden and uncontrollable ; there have to be intermediaries between them to control and regulate the movement. Even here, you see, there are intermediaries between the principle which gives the initial impetus and the organs which carry out a command or indicate a result. And there are a lot of other mechanisms in a watch which can also be seen in the human body. Anyone who knows how to observe and reason properly will recognize this great truth in the fields of physics, chemistry, biology, geography, history, sociology and psychology... absolutely everywhere.

If the physical body or the earth is to be transformed, there must, first of all, be contact, communication with the world of the spirit, with Heaven or, if you prefer, with Plato's world of Ideas, that is to say, with the intelligible world, the world of archetypes. And, for me, this is nothing less than the divine world. These channels of communication pass through the soul : the spirit can only reach the domain of matter through the intermediary of the soul and, on the level of the human body, these correspond to the nervous and

circulatory systems. The nervous system is closer
to the domain of the spirit, and the circulatory
system is closer to matter. The nervous system is
analogous to the air which feeds fire, that is to say :
the spirit ; the circulatory system is analogous to
the water that nourishes the earth, that is to say :
the physical body. You must study these two intermediaries, air and water, which find their correspondence, on the physical plane, in thought and
feeling.

At the summit, therefore, is the spirit which influences thought. Thought is more material than the
spirit ; also, it is always closely associated with feeling. If you think, for example, that a friend of yours
is becoming really harmful and dangerous to you,
your feelings towards him will change, you will no
longer be so fond of him. On the other hand, if you
discover that the friendship of someone for whom
you have never felt any special affection could be
very beneficial, that it is Providence that has
brought you together for your own good, you will
begin to love him. One's feelings vary, therefore,
according to one's thoughts ; I am sure you have
all experienced this time and again ; and once your
feelings are involved, they urge you to act, for feelings always need to express themselves in acts. You
are thinking of a woman : if you have no special
feeling for her, you will perhaps think that she is
pretty, perhaps even very beautiful, but that is all :

you will leave her alone. But then your feelings get involved and, immediately, you begin to take the initiative ! Feelings don't waste time, they set your body in motion at once, and off you go to buy flowers for her, to court her, to kiss her ! Before your feelings were involved, even though you recognized that she was charming, really lovely, your reaction was : 'She's not for me !' But once your feelings are involved the situation changes, for they are closely related to matter and express themselves materially by setting in motion a chain of reactions.

Don't try to touch matter directly by means of thought ; you won't succeed. Thought is principally designed to guide us, to enable us to know and to understand ; it cannot affect matter unless the heart is also involved. As long as feeling and desire have not been aroused you will do nothing. Oh, of course, you may sometimes do things that are dictated by reason, but you will do them without conviction or pleasure. Some people never feel anything and they still act. Yes, but they act like automatons. Whereas, when feelings are involved, it is a very different matter ! This does not necessarily mean that actions inspired by feelings are any better. Often, in fact, they are worse, for people sometimes do things without understanding why ; all they know is that their feelings are urging them to act and they hurry to obey the urge.

There are still a great many details that I have not explained ; I have restricted my explanations to the essentials, because I want to be sure that you understand the question clearly. The main thing to remember is that thought is a power, but that this power has to be properly understood. As long as you have not prepared the tool, the intermediary, the lever, the arm, it is no good believing that your thoughts will materialize on the physical plane ; they will continue to float in the rarer atmosphere of the mental plane. They will be recorded, to be sure, but they will not produce any material results. Whereas, if you bring them down onto the plane of feeling, they will always produce results.

And now, let's look at the question of hypnotism. You give someone who is under hypnosis a piece of paper, saying, 'It's a rose. Smell it and tell me what you smell.' And the person will talk to you about the exquisite perfume of that rose. This is because he is in a hypnotic state in which thought materializes instantly, not on the physical plane, but on the mental plane. The subject has picked up your thought, because your thought and the words that accompanied it have actually formed a rose on the mental plane and, as he is no longer functioning on the physical plane, his sense of smell is subtler and can pick up a perfume that exists only on the mental plane. He really and truly smells the rose,

therefore ; he is not mistaken. Or again, you can
give someone under hypnosis a glass of water and
tell him to drink it, saying, 'Here's a glass of brandy.
It's going to make you drunk', and, sure enough,
he drinks it and it really does make him drunk.
What has happened ? In this case, again, he is functioning on another plane and, on that plane, the
water really is brandy. This proves that the power
of thought is absolute and immediate, but on the
mental plane.

Knowing this, you can build anything, accomplish anything, in a flash, but in the higher
regions, not on the level of matter. Do you want
mansions, parks, gardens, cars, dancing girls, singing birds ? Whatever you want you can have, immediately. If you were a little more clairvoyant you
would actually see them, for they are already a reality. You will object, 'But there's nothing there ; I
can't touch anything !' Ah, if you want to touch
them, of course, it may well take several hundred
more years ! This is how you must understand the
question.

You can do all kinds of experiments in this area.
Suppose, for example, that there is a vicious wind
blowing. You can say a few honeyed words to it
to persuade it to be less harsh : 'How sweet and
gentle you are ! You're not wicked, on the contrary : you give me great pleasure !' and, after a
few minutes... Oh, to be sure, it is not the wind that

changes, it is you. Something in you changes, and the buffeting of the wind seems to you like the caresses of a lover ! You have to know how to pronounce the right words and do a little auto-suggestion, but people forget to pronounce the necessary words and they think that auto-suggestion is lies and illusion. No, no ; your suggestions are creations, subtle creations ; you pick up something with your subtle antennae and your antennae transmit it to your skin or your taste-buds, that is to say to the sensitive cells of your physical body. A great many people can be influenced by suggestion in this way, even perfectly normal people. You would be astounded to learn how often people are influenced by suggestion ! Yes, whole crowds. A man with a strong, clearly defined thought and a very powerful brain can say that something is thus and so and, immediately, everyone begins to feel the same thing. History is full of cases of this kind !

And now you must draw some conclusions : work with thought, but don't expect your thought to be realized immediately on the physical plane. You will say, 'Sometimes it is ; sometimes I only have to say a few words to change my frame of mind completely.' That is true but, as I have just explained, the change has not occurred on the level of matter and crystallized forms, but on the astral and mental levels, and you have picked it up on those levels. So the change can certainly be immediate, but on a higher level. And if you yourself are on that higher level then, of course, your thought is immediately effective.

As a matter of fact, thought can be materialized immediately on the physical level also. Some magicians are capable of producing or calming a storm, of causing or healing a disease, but this is because they have already worked to build the 'roads and bridges'. I certainly don't advise any of you to start trying to exert your power of thought directly on matter. Work with the power of thought, yes, but on a higher level, by asking for all that is most beneficial for your own evolution and that of the whole world. If you do that you may be sure of results... And then arm yourselves with patience and be ready to wait !

My faith and trust are not based on a vacuum, on illusion, but on Science. Everything I believe, everything I hope for, everything I do is founded on knowledge, and you can enter, in all tranquillity, into this knowledge. If you don't get the results you hoped for, don't say that it is because all that you have learned is false, check your own equipment to see if there is not something missing somewhere along the line. You will never be able to get your car moving if something is missing from the engine. Your watch will never keep time if its works are full of dust : you will have to get it cleaned. So, if something is not working as it should in your machinery, it is not the fault of the Science ; it is perhaps your own grasp of it that is incomplete.

Once you have understood this, great possibilities for creation will be wide open to you. For the creations of the spirit are true creations. You cannot see them ? That doesn't matter : don't bother about the question of whether you can see them or not. The only thing that matters is that they are real. And by believing that they are real you will be hastening their incarnation in the world of matter. Yes, if you really know these truths very thoroughly, you can greatly facilitate the work of all the luminous spirits in the world, the work in which, one day, you are all destined to participate fully and consciously. If your work has been ineffectual so far, it is because you were not ready, the intermediaries were not in place or you had not perfected them sufficiently ; perhaps you did not even know about them, and how can one work with something one knows nothing about ? But now that you are aware of the existence and importance of these intermediaries you will be able, in the fullness of faith, to develop and perfect them, and then you will be capable of fantastic creations.

A certain number of you have already begun to create, but your creations are still unstable, weedy little hybrids, because you are not really very convinced or very conscious of what you are doing, and your thoughts wander in all directions. There are days when you are more aware, more attuned to your divine ideal and more determined to live in harmony with it. But there are other days when you think, 'Well, I'll see about it. I'm going to allow myself a little treat today. Tomorrow I'll get back onto the straight and narrow...' Do as you please, but don't be surprised if your thought produces no effect.

You will ask, 'How do we go about getting in touch with the world of the spirit ?' Well, I spoke to you earlier about antennae which picked up waves and vibrations, and told you that man possessed antennae, spiritual antennae. But, whereas the physical antennae of radios and television sets remain fixed in one place, our spiritual antennae are mobile, extremely mobile, in fact, because they are alive. They are like a series of tuning forks in which each branch, depending on its length, vibrates in response to the wavelengths to which it is tuned, with which it has an affinity. You can illustrate this with an experiment of your own : arrange a series of tuning forks of different lengths in such a way that they can vibrate, and then play different notes on the piano. For each note you play, the fork that is in perfect affinity with the wave that strikes it will vibrate in response. And this is what happens with man. If he wants to pick up waves from Heaven he has to shorten the branches of his antennae ; the

longer they are, the more he will receive waves from
the lower worlds, even from Hell itself. So it
depends on man himself to make contact and
vibrate to the wavelengths he chooses and to which
he adjusts his antennae. Now, of course, when I
speak of lengthening or shortening your antennae,
it is a manner of speaking ; you can use any other
image you like to express the idea that man can be
more spiritual or more materialistic. The more
materialistic a man is, the more he receives communications from the lower regions ; the subtler and
more spiritual he is, the more intense his life
becomes and the more closely he is tuned to the
wavelength of Heaven. It all depends on him, for
he possesses every possibility within himself.

This is an immense field of work, open to all
those who want to become true creators.

Bear in mind, therefore, that thought is all-
powerful, but in its own domain, that is to say, on
the mental plane for, as thought is a highly subtle
matter, it can only fashion something instantaneous-
ly if it consists of equally subtle matter. If you desire
a palace, a mountain, a river, a child or a flower,
your thought becomes reality at once, but in its own
sphere. To be materialized it will have to descend
to a lower level. And, as thought always has a
tendency to become material, it begins by going
down to work on the astral level where it clothes
itself in slightly denser raiment. Then it gradually

becomes denser as it moves down to the etheric plane and, little by little, to the physical plane, where it materializes visibly and tangibly.

This mechanism of the psychic life of man is admirably expressed in the image of the sun which can only act on the earth and model it through the intermediary of air and water. If you fully understand this process, you will be capable of wonderful achievements. The entire science of white magic and theurgy is contained in this image of the four elements : sun, air, water and earth.

6

STRIKING A BALANCE
BETWEEN MATTER AND THE SPIRIT

Man has tremendous possibilities for action on the physical level, but his possibilities on the psychic level are even greater. The only trouble is, though, that he has never exercised his possibilities in the domain of thought, and he does not know how to exploit them. One constantly meets people whose first reaction in the face of an unexpected difficulty is to panic or give way to despair ! The possibility that their thought, their spirit, might possess elements with which they could remedy the situation never seems to occur to them. No, they start running round in circles, weeping and gnashing their teeth and looking for a solution in medication... or guns ! And that is why everything goes from bad to worse !

The first thing to do when you meet a difficulty is to concentrate, to enter into yourself and make contact with the invisible world, so as to be given the light to see what you should do. This is the only way to be sure of acting lucidly, efficiently and with method. Of course, there is nothing to prevent you from resorting to material means as well, but you must not begin with them ; you must begin with the psychic means. How can you expect to correct a difficult situation if you lose your head and cannot see where you are going ? That is the best possible way to confuse and destroy everything. And it is often what happens : people act blindly, without thinking ; they lose their heads so completely in a fire that, instead of escaping, they throw themselves into the flames !

You will never find the solutions you need without light. Take an example : if you are woken in the middle of the night by a noise — something has fallen and broken, or someone has got into your house — do you rush out in the dark to see what it was ? No, you know that that would be dangerous. Your first reaction is to switch on the light, then you can see what woke you up and do something about it. And this applies in every circumstance in life : the first thing to do is to throw light on the situation. In other words : the first thing to do is to concentrate and reflect so as to see what action to take. If you have no light you will wander in different directions, knock on different doors and try all kinds of ineffectual means. Yes, simply because you have no light. The essential factor is light ; thanks to the light you will avoid wasting a great deal of time and money and doing a lot of damage.

Those who are in the habit of giving priority to the inner life, to thought, the will, the spirit, always have greater self-mastery and power ; they are always more serene and fulfilled than others. These are commonly known facts which are easily verifiable, but they have always been overlooked by science and left to psychologists or mystics to study. Orthodox science should have studied this question a long time ago, for anything that goes on in man is far too important to be neglected. The methods that have enabled Initiates and Sages to triumph over all their tribulations, the elements they used and where they acquired these elements, all this should already have been studied in detail, but it never has, and the result is an immense gap in scientific knowledge. The day will come when men call science to account for not having examined this question.

Human beings possess extremely effective inner faculties of thought, imagination and will but, obviously, as they habitually prefer to have recourse to external means, they have not developed their psychic faculties. They have no faith — or perhaps it is simply that they lack patience — so they are always looking for tangible, external, material solutions. 'Oh, thought !' they say ; 'I've tried it and it didn't work !' And why didn't it work ? Suppose you have a physical or psychic failing of some kind : it took you centuries to develop and reinforce it, so is it any wonder that you cannot get rid of it just like that, in a couple of minutes ? It may take centuries more to undo all that ! There is such a thing as justice in the universe.

As a matter of fact, the best way is to combine the two, the inner and the outer means ; you will get things done more rapidly that way, but you must begin by working with the soul, the spirit and thought, before adding the physical element that will facilitate the process. At the moment you do just the opposite : science makes all kinds of discoveries which technology and industry apply, and this makes the economic wheels of the country go round. In the interests of the economy, the human race is being poisoned and its health undermined. The human race is being sacrificed to the aggrandizement of science !

Do you think that I am exaggerating ? No, not really. A great deal of work is being done for the progress of science, and not much for the progress of human beings. If you want your kiln to stay hot you have to keep feeding fuel into it. Well, the fuel that is being used to keep the fires of science burning are human beings. Thanks to its human victims, the kiln of science is always hot. Fifty years from now there will not be a single healthy man on the planet. And when I say fifty years I am being optimistic. You are advised to drink this and swallow that, and this is how you become intoxicated. Well, the advice I give you is to take no medication of any kind ; eat properly, breathe properly, work properly and sleep properly and, above all, think properly ! But I know very well that I could talk about this for centuries, and there would never be more than a few to follow my advice. The majority would say, 'What rubbish ! Can you imagine ? Have recourse to the inner world, to thought... No, no. We know what to do !' and they would continue to look for everything they need outside themselves.

Yes, it can truly be said that, because of all the instruments and machines that science puts at the disposal of human beings, they are gradually losing the use of their faculties, for they no longer have to make an effort or do any inner work. If this continues, things will never improve ; if they do nothing to shake themselves out of their present state of spiritual lethargy and paralysis, the recourse to external means can only make their inner forces weaker and weaker. Outwardly, their standard of living seems to be improving, but the inner reality is a continual erosion of will-power and vitality. As a matter of fact, certain thinkers and scientists have already begun to express their doubts about whether technical progress really contributes to the good of humanity.

Does this mean that progress should be halted ? No, it is Nature herself that has given men the urge to continue their researches : they must never stop searching, never stop delving deeper and deeper into the mysteries of Nature. But their work should have a different goal, it must be steered in a different direction, upwards, towards the spirit, the inner life.

The truth is that men have never understood the true reason for technical progress. Have all these tools, instruments, machines and mechanical means of locomotion been invented so that human beings need never make an effort — not even the effort of walking on their own two feet — since there is always a machine to do everything for them ? No, all these technical improvements are there to allow them to free themselves from the daily grind of their material tasks and dedicate more time to spiritual, divine activities. This is the true significance of technical progress : to set men free for other kinds of work. If it is not used for this purpose it is very bad ; it is very bad for man to have nothing more to do than laze about on the beach and stagnate and moulder away, while machines do all his work for him. It is important to understand that Cosmic Intelligence permits all this material progress so that man may, at last, free himself from his prosaic work and devote himself to sublime activities.

Now, I want to get you to explore your own inner world. When you have a difficulty, sorrow or suffering of any kind, say to yourselves, 'I can put that right. I'll soon bring back the smiles, the joy and gladness' ; and you will succeed just as long as you recognize, in advance, that you have the power to do so. There are moments in your life when you are perfectly happy, you feel that you have everything you desire, that nothing is lacking to you and then, the very next moment, you feel forlorn and destitute. Perhaps you think that the first feeling, the sense of happiness, was an illusion. No, it was a reality, but a reality of another kind, of a kind that you don't appreciate. It is when you are convinced — wrongly — that you have nothing, that you are deluding yourself ; you are blind to all that invisible reality in and around you. The question is to determine what you need and then to discover that, in fact, you already have it, within you.

Let me illustrate this : a pauper living in an attic complains that he is poor, abandoned, downtrodden. I tell him, 'Don't you know who your father and mother were ? Don't you know that they bequeathed you a rich inheritance ? Why do you shut yourself up in this place ? Look at all those fields and lakes and forests, all those great mansions ; they are all yours ; enjoy them !' So then he begins to explore, and what does he find ? He finds that he has great and magnificent possessions. He did not know that he was heir to all that ! Well, the same thing happens when you begin to explore all the inner possibilities you possess : they are infinite, but

you don't realize it, and that is where the problem
lies. Obviously, I am not talking about the external
world. The external world doesn't belong to you,
that is true, but inwardly everything belongs to you.
Yes, on the inner level the universe itself belongs
to you ; you lack absolutely nothing ; it is all yours.
Go and look at it, explore it and enjoy it all, for
you are all heirs of the Heavenly Father and of
Mother Nature. How can you still have the impression that you are poor and underprivileged ?

To be sure, I am not saying that you must totally
neglect the material aspect. I am not preaching the
abandonment of everything but meditation and
prayer, as some yogis or Christian ascetics have
done. Our goal is different, it does not consist in
winning a handful of people and leading them on
a purely spiritual, mystic path. Our goal is to win
the whole world, and you cannot lead the whole
world on a path that was only intended for the few.
And, since our aims are different, our methods must
also be different. It was all right when a few her-
mits and ascetics disappeared into the forests and
deserts, but to think that the populations of whole
countries should do the same, each person praying
and meditating under his own little tree or in his
own little grotto... what utter nonsense ! Who
would do the work ? Who would take care of growing enough food for everyone to have the
minimum ? Everyone would have to be prepared

to die of hunger and cold ! No, my purpose is to give men a philosophical system that can be applied by everyone : each person must be free to work, earn his living, marry and have a family but, at the same time, each one should have an inner light, a discipline, a method of work.

It is a question of giving both the spiritual and the material dimension their due ; so far very few have ever really reached this ideal. Some, in their desire to shun the world with all its temptations and difficulties, have chosen to spend their lives meditating in solitude, but the majority have always been totally absorbed by worldly affairs. The important thing is to combine the two : to live a divine life and to live it in the world. In myself, these two aspects are harmoniously combined and it is up to you, now, to achieve this harmony, for you are still at the stage where, if you begin to take an interest in the spiritual life, you let all your worldly interests go to ruin or, if you are interested in worldly affairs, your spiritual life deteriorates. It should not be like that : you must have both. Believe me, it is possible !

Thanks to all the explanations I give you, you are beginning to feel that your life has meaning and direction, that you know where you are going. This means that you will receive more and more light as well as more and more joy and happiness, for they go hand in hand. As long as you believe yourselves

to be poor and disinherited, you will be unhappy :
if you suddenly discovered that your house contained hidden treasure, don't you think that it would
make a difference ? Of course it would ! And it will
be the same when you discover your inner riches
and possibilities, all your inner force. You will immediately be full of smiles.

7

THE STRENGTH OF THE SPIRIT

Most human beings feel the need to dominate others and impose their own will, and for this reason they want to be strong and powerful. Yes, but where do they look for the power they need ? In machines, weapons and every kind of material equipment external to themselves. And, of course, they appear to find it there for, when they have these things, they are free to impose their will on others, to use violence and wreak destruction. But that is not where true strength lies. You may feel very strong when you have machines, planes, missiles, machine guns or atomic bombs, but all those things are external : where would all your strength be if they were taken away ? If you feel strong because of all the things you possess, your strength is an illusion ; are you yourself any more capable of carrying a heavy weight, of throwing a stone farther, of freeing yourself from certain kinds of suffering or difficulty ? No, you are not. So your strength is not really yours. You enjoy certain external means, but what would happen to you if you lost them ?

Initiates have understood for ages that, instead
of spending their lives trying to acquire powers that
would never really be theirs, they would do better
to work to acquire true inner powers. This is what
they are constantly striving for, this is their true
work. They know that true strength lies within, in
that inner being who thinks, feels and acts. And this
is why they have laid down certain rules and
methods to enable that being in whom all power is
invested, the spirit, to manifest itself fully, perfectly
and absolutely. It is to the spirit that man must turn
to find power. True power, true strength is in the
spirit, in the will and intelligence of the spirit.

Take just one example : everyone is lost in admiration before an electronic microscope capable
of enlarging something 100,000 times, but they
forget the one thing that is essential : they forget
that they could not see anything at all if they did
not have eyes ; without eyes all the microscopes in
the world would be useless ! Why are they so full
of praise for an external instrument when, in reality,
all the merit and glory belong to the being who
sees ? And who is this being ? The spirit. It is the
spirit that sees through our eyes ; it is not the eyes
that are the essential, it is the being that uses them,
the spirit. But nobody pays any attention to the
spirit ; it is completely ignored.

This mistaken attitude is the result of the
materialistic philosophy which has misled men by

making them turn away from their inner reality and lose themselves so completely in the mists of matter that they no longer recognize the fundamental truths that would enable them to solve their problems.

It is important to understand this : nothing external can ever really belong to us ; it is only lent to us for a very limited period and we shall never find true strength in it. True strength is to be found only in the being that creates all those external things, that is to say, in the spirit that manifests itself outwardly. Proof of this can be seen when the spirit leaves a man for, although all his organs may still be intact, they have stopped functioning ; the stomach no longer digests, the heart no longer beats, the lungs have ceased to breathe and the brain to reason. If you weigh him you will find that he is just as heavy as before, nothing has changed ; and yet he is dead ! Yes, because the essential factor, the being that once lived, thought and felt within him, is no longer there.

The essential, the only thing that counts, is life, the spirit. What is the point of pursuing nonessentials ? It would be true to say that the real difference between an Initiate and an ordinary person is precisely this : the Initiate is only concerned with what is essential. He seeks the spirit, he seeks to give the spirit every opportunity to develop and blossom and manifest all the riches hidden within it.

Look at a cell : it is composed of the membrane, the cytoplasm and the nucleus. Similarly, we are composed of a body, a soul and a spirit. This is why Initiatic Science sees man's body as the 'skin' of the soul ; his soul as the cytoplasm in which the forces and energies of life circulate, and the spirit as the nucleus, the focal point of intelligence that creates, orders and organizes the whole. It is the nucleus that creates by means of the cytoplasm ; the cytoplasm provides the nucleus with the matter it needs, but power resides in the nucleus. Similarly, in man, it is the spirit that seeks to manifest itself and provide the impetus so as to create new forms and fashion matter. Man has reached his present stage of development thanks to the efforts the spirit has made to manifest itself through matter.

When you are inspired, when you feel that an inner force is urging you to do something noble, to help others and become one with the Universal Soul, it is the spirit that is manifesting itself in you. When, on the contrary, you feel empty and assailed by doubt and discouragement, when you are tempted to abandon everything, it is because matter has gained the upper hand in you and is opposing the efforts of the spirit. What can you do when this happens ? You can call on the intellect to remedy the situation.

The intellect has the power to intervene because it lies on the threshold between the spirit and matter, or rather, between the spirit and the heart. When the intellect sees that matter has gained the upper hand and is opposing the divine impulse of the spirit, it can act to reinforce the spirit and clear away the obstacles in its path. The spirit never relaxes its thrust from within, but man is not conscious of it and does not know that he can facilitate its work or, on the contrary, oppose it by giving greater leeway to matter. If all Initiates found schools, it is precisely with this in mind : to teach human beings to work at perfecting their own being, to teach them to control and purify themselves so as to allow the spirit to manifest itself. If man did not have the capacity to act by means of his intellect and will, Initiates would never have tried to urge him to become aware of his role in the universe ; everything would have taken place without him. But man does have a role to play in the evolution of creation and God does take him into account. If God created man it was for this very reason : that he should contribute to the cosmic work.

God gave inertia to matter and impetus to the spirit and man is situated between the two. Outwardly he is enveloped in matter, but inwardly he is immersed in the immensity of the spirit. He receives this twofold influence, therefore : at times it is the spirit that manifests itself through him and at times it is matter that attempts to imprison him and drag him back into the primeval chaos. He is constantly obliged to struggle, therefore, and if he is unenlightened and inactive he sinks into a state of inertia. This is what happens to those who never do any intellectual, spiritual, divine work : matter gets the upper hand in them and they become foul-smelling sewers, swamps full of tadpoles, frogs and mosquitoes.

A disciple, who has someone to enlighten and guide him, does nothing to oppose the spirit ; on the contrary, he opens all his doors to it, and when the spirit is enthroned as king, it sets to work to harmonize, embellish, illuminate, vivify and resuscitate his whole being. And these transformations can be accomplished very rapidly once the spirit is given priority. Matter can only engulf, absorb and stifle life, whereas the spirit can organize, vivify and resuscitate ; in fact, it can do nothing else : that is why it must be given priority. How many human beings have become blocks of stone because they prevented the spirit from manifesting itself in them !

But, let's carry our investigation a little further : since all power is invested in the spirit but can only manifest itself through the medium of matter, it is impossible to conceive of pure spirit totally apart from matter. If pure spirit exists it does not belong to our universe and we cannot know the region in which it exists. In our universe, spirit and matter are linked ; everything we see and touch consists of spirit and matter combined in one form or another.

Take the example of nuclear fission : people imagine that it is matter that produces the explosion. No, the matter is only the form that contains, grips and compresses the spirit. In reality, an atomic explosion is an eruption of the spirit manifesting itself as fire, heat. For the explosion to take place, the spirit has to be there, compressed within matter, for matter alone can do nothing : it is simply a vehicle, a container. The spirit is volatile, if there were no matter to contain it, it would escape. Scientists are fascinated by the power of matter ; they have never realized that the energy released by matter is the energy of the spirit. For the time being, all this power is bottled up in matter in order to prevent it from escaping, but it is simply waiting for the opportunity to manifest itself. Proof of this can be seen in the fact that, once released, there is no way of getting it back ; once the spirit is released it is impossible to capture it again and it returns to where it came from. As for the matter that contained it, it is blown to dust, nothing is left of it, for the power of the spirit is such that, given the opportunity, it annihilates matter.

And what is a tree ? A tree is a reservoir, a stockpile of solar energy ; you only need to burn it to prove this. When you burn a tree, you are simply triggering a chain reaction of energy. It is the same phenomenon, in a different form, as that of nuclear fission. The energies trapped in the tree escape and, like prisoners breaking their bonds with a great rattling of chains and locks, as they escape, we hear the crackling of their shattered chains. This crackling is the sound of solar energies escaping from the wood in the form of heat which can be used by man. The water vapour, air and gasses rise, whereas the ashes, which are the part of earth contained in the tree, stay in your fireplace. As you can see, the quantity of ashes, compared to the water and gasses released, is relatively small ; and this is yet another proof that the matter of the tree held the spirit captive within it.

Where did the energy released by burning a tree first come from ? It was not actually produced by the tree ; the tree was only the material container in which it was stored. It came from the sun. Matter cannot produce energy ; energy comes from another region, and matter is only there to contain and preserve it.

Initiates, who have investigated all the different manifestations of life, wished to teach man methods by which he could recover his primeval power. For, in the beginning, he possessed great powers and the whole of nature obeyed him, but he lost them when he let himself be dragged down by the weight of matter ; this is what is known as the Fall : the fault which caused man to lose his powers by allowing them to be engulfed in a dense, coarser form of matter. Before the Fall, man already existed in matter, but in an etheric form of matter, by means of which he could accomplish wonders. This is why the Bible says that Adam and Eve lived in Paradise, in the Garden of Eden, in a state of nudity, purity and light ; at that time, illness and death were unknown to them.

In attempting to penetrate and explore the denser forms of matter, human beings lost their lightness, liberty and immortality. They became subject to disease and death. And today, thousands of years later, the story is still the same : suffering, illness and death. And it will continue to be the same until they set foot on the path leading back to their primeval way of life. This is what the Initiates call 'the reintegration of beings' : the return to the primitive state of glory. In fact, this is the whole philosophy of Initiates. They tell us : 'You are between the spirit and matter, so you must reflect and study yourselves and always know which of the two predominates in you. When you see the first sign of thoughts or feelings that tend to drag you down or torment you, instead of letting them have their way, you must try to neutralize them. Those who allow themselves to be subjugated by matter lose all their light, freedom and beauty, whereas those who manage to struggle free of matter and give priority to the spirit, become free, luminous and strong.'

Strength is in the spirit. This is why you must

penetrate more and more profoundly into yourselves in order to reach the divine spiritual principle within you. If you do this, a spring will begin to flow within you, and you will feel refreshed, sustained and flooded with inexhaustible energies. But if you neglect the spirit and concern yourselves exclusively with external things (money, houses, machines or arms), then power, the true power and strength of the spirit will abandon you. Why ? Because you give it no support or encouragement ; you never think of it or have recourse to it ; you are not in communion with it. With the remnants of strength left to you, you will be able to drag on for a time, but you will never get very far. You may think that you are very strong, but your springs will dry up because you have broken the connection with the spirit, and you will soon see if you are really so strong and powerful ! No : you will be rubbed out and swept away !

Most human beings rely exclusively on externals, but how long will these last ? During their lifetime, to be sure, they may have money and arms in plenty, but when the time comes for them to die, as they cannot take all that with them and as they have never done anything to reinforce their spirit, they will leave the earth with nothing ! When this happens they will understand that all their imaginary strength has vanished, and begin to suffer and regret the past ; and this is precisely what Hell is. Many come back amongst the living and try to talk to their wives or children, but no one can hear what they say. Others go to spiritualistic seances and speak through a medium in an attempt to warn the living not to live an empty, senseless life like theirs, but nobody pays any attention to them. And then, one day, they reincarnate and have to begin all over again from scratch, because thieves have made off with all the wealth they had amassed.

This gives you some idea of the disappointments in store for those who have never experienced Initiation : they are truly to be pitied. But what wealth is enjoyed by those who have worked to acquire faculties, virtues and qualities ! Even if they have no external possessions, they are rich in knowledge and strength, and when they leave for the next world, they take all that with them. Since they have worked to develop these qualities, they will be theirs for ever ; no one can take them away. In fact, in the next world, they will receive an abundance of all that they hoped and worked for on earth. Those who loved light and colour will be able to contemplate them endlessly. The stars and the whole universe will sing for those whose souls were full of music and symphonies. All the secrets of the universe will be revealed to those whose one desire was knowledge.

True strength is to be found in the spirit, for the qualities of the spirit have a special link with strength. Intelligence, wisdom and purity confer great powers. Love too ! If you have great love, you will also be capable of overcoming all your negative states : heartache, sorrow, anger and hatred... Yes, because love is an alchemist capable of transmuting everything. But true strength is to be found in truth, for truth is the veritable domain of the spirit.

Jesus said, 'You shall know the truth, and the truth shall make you free.' In order to be free one needs the true strength which wisdom alone does not possess ; a great many sages never found true freedom. And even love cannot free you completely all by itself. Only truth can do this ; in other words, only the union of love and wisdom. This is what Initiatic Science teaches. But men neglect love, they neglect wisdom, and they think that it is money that will set them free ! Never ! Money will enslave them, for it will give them every opportunity to feed their lower nature, to abandon themselves to pleasure, to give a free rein to every whim and even to revenge themselves by eliminating others if need be. In other words, money will set them on the path that leads to Hell ! Of course, for the wise, for those who are truly in control of themselves, money can help them to be free and do a great deal of good. But give money to the weak and you will see whether it frees them or not ! Outwardly, perhaps ; they will be able to shake off someone who was bothering them, they will be able to flee persecution, but inwardly they will be no freer from their own weaknesses, vices and mental torment. Money may enable them to get away from home, but wherever they go they will take all their ills with them. Very often, it is the wealthy who are held by the strongest bonds ; those who are poor and intelligent are far freer.

You will not understand this unless you put everything in its proper place, and this is what an Initiatic school can teach you. An Initiatic school will not teach you zoology, botany, ethnology, geography or history, but it will teach you the science of life. No subject is more neglected than this. There are schools for everything else, but where can you learn how to live ? Nowhere ! Except here... Yes, we are in one of those rare, exceptional schools which teach how to live : how to think, feel and act. Unfortunately, very few appreciate the true value of such a school ; the others will understand when it is already too late, when it is time for them to leave this earth.

At the moment, human beings are still a prey to the materialistic philosophy which has estranged them from true strength, and they are growing continually weaker. But a few years hence, you will see materialism banished and rejected and everywhere, in universities, schools and families, human beings will be taught the science of the spirit. Then they will realize that, for centuries, they have simply been marking time, and that all their technical and scientific discoveries do not really constitute progress. True progress is progress of the spirit ; there is no progress except that of the spirit. Write these words down, they constitute a formula for the future. New discoveries are being made all the time, but something that can only offer material well-being or physical comfort does not make human beings any better. On the contrary, they become more and more selfish and vindictive, more and more vulnerable and prone to disease and, at the same time, prouder, more conceited and more licentious. This is the fruit of our so-called progress ; it is not the progress of the spirit.

The progress of the spirit is to make human beings better, to improve their thoughts and feelings so that they may always be in good physical and psychic health, whereas the much-vaunted 'progress' of today consists largely in opening new and more sophisticated hospitals, clinics and prisons ! Instead of looking to the spirit for the remedy, instead of setting things straight inside themselves, everybody rushes to look for solutions on the outside. Nobody thinks of looking within for their solutions ; nobody, that is, except a few mystics and spiritualists whom everybody laughs at !

True strength comes from within, from the spirit, that is to say, from the centre. I do not deny that there are some useful elements at the periphery, but they are the least important. Authentic reality resides at the centre, in the spirit ; all the rest is more or less tainted or diluted and impure. Even gold and precious stones, which are the purest things nature produces, have to be extracted from their gangue of earth and stone. Anything that does not come directly from the source, that is out of touch with the centre, is mixed with impurities and has to be cleansed and decanted. Only those who drink directly at the fountainhead enjoy water that is absolutely pure.

In every corner of the universe and in every aspect of man the two principles of life and death manifest themselves. As soon as life strives to manifest itself, opposing forces arise and try to hold it down and destroy it, and life has to defend itself. It is a constant to and fro of action and reaction. And if man is not watchful he is in danger of being swept away by the forces of death. How many precious lessons can be learned from this truth !

A sister comes to see me, for instance, and tells me that she is disappointed and discouraged, that nothing seems to go right. Then I look at her and tell her, 'It is because you have joined the school of weakness.' 'What school do you mean, Master ?' she asks ; 'I went to school as a child, but I'm not going to school now.' I tell her, 'Yes, you are in the school of weakness', but as she still does not

understand, I explain : 'In the school of weakness
no one makes an effort, no one takes any exercise,
whether physical or spiritual ; everybody lounges
about in armchairs, interested only in comfort and
laziness. All right ; wonderful ! But what is the
result ? The result is that all inner movement slows
down too ; the intensity of life, of thought and of
the spirit is diminished, and this leaves the door open
to negative elements which slip in and leave dirty
footmarks and impurities which you do not know
how to get rid of. Life must be lived with intensity
in order to dispel all the filth that keeps trying to
sneak in and create problems within you. Put
yourself down for the school of strength ; in other
words, maintain a high level of activity, vigilance,
dynamic energy, courage and enthusiasm.'

Knowing that the two principles of life and death
are constantly at war within you, you must not
abandon the struggle and allow negative forces to
invade you and shackle you. To begin with, it may
be pleasant to let oneself go, but one ends by being
paralysed : one's blood and all one's cells, every part
of one, simply stops vibrating and can no longer
resist or struggle against the inevitable invasion of
dust, mould and mildew. When a wheel spins very
fast, mud cannot stick to it, it is flung off at every
turn, but as soon as the wheel slows down it begins
to be clogged with mud. Have you understood ?
There is a wonderful philosophy and the most ex-

traordinary science hidden here. So it is up to you, now, to make an effort, for it is very much in your own interest to avoid becoming soft and lazy. You have to exercise every part of your being : your limbs and lungs, your thoughts and emotions, your soul and your spirit. If you do this you will be maintaining a vibratory state of such intensity that it will reject all impurities and you will be able to keep moving forward for a very long time.

For years I have been telling you : 'Get a move on ! Go and sign up in the school for strength. Make an effort !' Yes, because inactivity is lethal. One day you will find out for yourselves that it is vital to live with intensity. This is why your lives must be marked by enthusiasm ; this is why you must never abandon love, spiritual love, for it is love that creates the state of outpouring and radiance which alone is capable of rejecting everything negative and obscure. Those who pride themselves on being intelligent and wise, and think that love and kindness are pointless, have signed their own death warrant... for their spiritual death, first of all, but the other kind of death will follow before long.

You must make up your minds, today, to understand the meaning of life, health and strength. Strength is to be found in the activity of the spirit.

8

SOME RULES FOR SPIRITUAL WORK

It is not success that matters in the eyes of Heaven, but the efforts you make, for only your efforts will keep you on the right path ; your successes may often lead you to relax your vigilance. It does not matter if you don't succeed, if you have nothing to show for your work : at least you have worked.

Don't look for success, therefore. In any case, success does not depend on you but on Heaven, and Heaven will give it to you when the time is ripe. The only thing that depends on you are your own efforts, for Heaven cannot make them for you. Just as no one else can eat in your place, Heaven cannot eat for you either, that is to say, Heaven cannot make an effort for you ; it is you that have to do that. But Heaven gives success as and when It pleases, according to what is best for your evolution. Countless saints, prophets and Initiates have left this world without having succeeded ! In spite of their light, integrity and purity, their ideal failed to win through, which proves that success did not depend on them.

Some of you often worry about this. You say, 'I pray and meditate, and yet nothing ever changes. Why ?' The truth is that a great deal changes, great transformations are constantly taking place, but they are so subtle that you cannot see them. So, don't lose courage ! Sacred Scripture says that God is faithful and true. Every effort you make to fashion and gain control of your inner matter, all the work you do in order to spiritualize it so that your presence may be more and more beneficial for the whole world... all this is recorded and, one day, you will see the results. When ? Ah, that is the one question that is hard to answer, but you should not worry about it ; all you have to do is keep up your work and leave it to Heaven to decide when, where and how your efforts will be rewarded.

As a matter of fact, the efforts themselves contain their own reward. Every time you make an effort, with every mental exercise, life takes on another colour, another flavour. If Initiates get so much joy and happiness from the least little thing, it is because of all their previous spiritual work. If they had not done this work they would be just like all those blasé, disillusioned people who have everything and are bored by it, who have lost all their zest for life because there is no inner activity, no intensity of spiritual life.

Even if you do not see any immediate results, you can be sure that nothing is more effective than this work. If the results are slow in coming it is because the spiritual, divine world is harder to reach than the material world, but that is no reason to abandon your work. If you abandon it, it shows that you possess neither science nor discernment. How long does it take to grow a lettuce ? And an oak tree ? Yes, but how long will a lettuce last ? And how long will an oak tree last ? In the inner life the laws are exactly the same : if you want a lettuce (symbolically speaking), you can have it in no time at all, but it will soon wilt ; whereas, if you want an oak tree you are going to have to wait a long time, but it will live for centuries.

So, the only answer is to keep working ! Never try to fix a deadline for the achievement of your spiritual aspirations. If you make up your mind that, by such and such a date, you will have reached a particular spiritual goal or overcome a particular failing, you will only succeed in becoming tense and disrupting the harmony of your development. You must work toward perfection, but without giving yourself a deadline ; tell yourself that you have all eternity before you and that, one day, you will reach the perfection you long for. The only thing you should think about is the beauty of the work you have undertaken. Tell yourself, 'It's so beautiful that I'm not worried about how many hundreds or thousands of years it's going to take me to get there !'

Many spiritualists think that once they have made up their minds about something, everything will come to pass exactly as they want it to, that their instincts will obey them and wisdom and reason will triumph. They don't think about all those other forces that may be aroused and prevent them from reaching their goal and, when they realize that they have failed in what they set out to achieve or that they have not done so as quickly as they had hoped, they become embittered and angry and pester everyone with their frustrated ambitions. One should never launch into the spiritual life without knowing the rules, because the results could be worse than if one had continued to interest oneself only in one's prosaic occupations.

In fact, generally speaking, one should never have too much self-confidence when undertaking any spiritual activity, for an excessively self-assured attitude can cause other forces to react and oppose the realization. You must have already noticed this : you promise someone that you will do such and such a thing for him on such and such a day and, when the day comes, you no longer have the slightest desire to keep your promise. And yet, when you committed yourself, you were sincere ; you had every intention of keeping your word. Henceforth, therefore, don't make too many promises ; don't tell everybody what you plan to do ; keep your hopes and desires to yourself. In this way, fewer obstacles will crop up to prevent them from being realized. It is very important to know this.

A disciple must not embark on the spiritual life without possessing certain notions in advance, otherwise he may have some very unpleasant surprises. A human being can be compared to a tree. Yes, like a tree, a human being has roots, a trunk and branches which bear leaves, flowers and fruit. The taller the tree, the deeper its roots ; in other words, the higher a human being rises, the more his deep instinctive tendencies — sensuality, anger, pride, etc. — are likely to be aroused.

It is important to know human nature and to know that, when you set something in motion in one part of your being, it will automatically trigger a reaction in another part. You will say, 'Well, if it means that by dedicating myself to the spiritual life I'll only succeed in reinforcing my instincts, it would be better not to do so !' No, there are ways of overcoming and controlling these forces and using them to obtain even greater inner achievements. This is what is known as spiritual alchemy. Yes, there are many things one needs to know in order not to get lost !

And if you do win a victory, be careful not to rest on your laurels ; you must be even more vigilant than before, because opposing forces may attack you and, if you are taken off guard, you might well lose the advantage you had gained. These are laws : everything is connected and a movement in one area necessarily provokes a reaction in the opposite area. This is why, when an Initiate is engaged in a very luminous activity for the benefit of mankind, he cannot avoid awakening and provoking a reaction from the opposite forces, the forces of darkness. But, as he is well aware of this, he takes the necessary precautions. The fact that one arouses the hostility of the forces of darkness is not a reason to refrain from working for the light. Here again, you must learn how to stand up to these forces and go on working until you reach the final victory ; at the same time, you must learn how to use difficulties as a stimulus in your work.

But, above all, a disciple must never forget that, in the spiritual life it is not up to him to decide when he is going to achieve his goal otherwise, when his most elevated aspirations fail to materialize on time he will be discouraged or embittered and abandon the whole thing. What a pity it would be to give up all his efforts, just because success took longer than he expected ! No, you must continue to work in plenitude, splendour and peace, for this is the only way to come, one day, to perfection.

9

THE WEAPONS OF THOUGHT

I

There are all kinds of exercises that you can do with thought. Suppose, for instance, that you have a difficult problem : instead of letting it defeat you, put it side by side with all the good things you have, all the riches and possibilities within you, and compare them. You will see that your difficulty will not be able to stand the comparison ; in the face of your immense wealth it will fade into nothing. Yes, learn to bring your sorrows and distress face to face with your true riches, the future that is in store for you, your ideal, and you will see that they will disappear without a trace. This is the method of confrontation, and you must learn to use it : it is extremely effective. One often sees examples of this in life : little by little, the person who is not being entirely truthful begins to feel guilty, to hesitate and stammer, and finally gives in and surrenders, whereas his opponent, although he may have seemed weaker and smaller in the beginning, if he has truth on his side, will gradually become stronger and begin to hold his head up. Where does his strength come from ? From his sense of being in the right. And the stronger he becomes, the more uncomfortable his opponent feels. To begin with he will bluster and threaten and try to hide his embarrassment in face of the truth and then, all of a sudden, he will collapse like a pricked balloon.

And whenever you are being plagued by troublesome entities, tell them, 'Come here, I want to show you something', and then bring them face to face with all the wealth you already possess and all that will be yours in the future. They will begin by trying to bluff and bluster, but they will soon disappear without a trace and you will realize that, in this way, you can transform and improve a great many things. Why not practise doing this ? Life is full of experiences of this kind that you can try ; there is never any need to be bored, there is always some interesting experiment you can do, something useful to be learned or to create.

Then again, if you are visited by malevolent entities who try to convince you that you are barking up the wrong tree by embracing the spiritual life, you can confront these inner enemies with the beauty and depth of your spiritual experiences : they will be left speechless and will turn tail and leave you in peace. And if they come back again, later, adopt the same attitude : receive them politely and gently and tell them, 'Yes, I understand what you're saying but tell me : how is it that I have experienced such sublime moments and understood all these things ?' Then you give them a detailed account of all that you have received. They will be put to flight in no time !

Entities like these have visited the greatest geniuses, artists, thinkers and philosophers, and even the greatest saints and Initiates, in the hope of upsetting them and getting them to abandon their work. And, very often, they have succeeded ! Even Jesus was not spared this experience : remember the three temptations in the desert. But, as you know, they failed to convince him, he answered Satan by quoting the great truths of the Bible to him, and it was Satan who surrendered.

And countless entities tried to tempt Jesus at the last moment, in the Garden of Gethsemani, telling him, 'You're not obliged to submit to this destiny. You can still avoid being put to death. You've already done so much, do you think that it is really necessary to sacrifice your life ? Besides, look at these men you are trying to save : they don't appreciate you ; they've already betrayed you. Go on ; get away while you can !' And Jesus came very close to giving way to temptation. But then, he suddenly pulled himself up and answered them : 'Away with you ! This is the mission I have come to accomplish and I must go through with it !' and the evil entities were defeated and left him alone. But what anguish they put him through !

Yes, these entities try to tempt everybody ; not only you, but also the greatest prophets and the greatest saints. Doubt, the fear of death, sensuality, pride... how many temptations there are ! A great many saints were tempted by pride. The Enemy told them, 'You're too strong for me, you've completely vanquished me ! What a will, what power ! What mighty weapons you have !' He hoped that he could get them to respond with pride, that they would say, 'Ah yes, Evil One, I have vanquished you ; I'm very strong !' But those who were instructed in Initiatic Science were on their guard ; they replied, 'No, it was not I who vanquished you ; it was the Christ within me who vanquished you !' and in saying this they overcame the temptation.

You see : you must always know what to say, how to answer. The word 'dialogue' is in fashion these days, but an inner dialogue with these inferior entities — a regular set-to, in fact — has always existed ! If you know what answer to give, by which I mean, if you know how to do some serious mental work, you will be the winner ; and if you don't know how to do that, you will be the loser ! So, learn to reply as Jesus replied : 'Man shall not live by bread alone but by every word of God' ; 'You shall not tempt the Lord your God', and, 'You shall worship the Lord your God, and Him only shall you serve.' Take hold of these truths, they are the true weapons you need in order to repel the spirits of evil. Grasp them and use them against your enemies ; only the truth is all-powerful and capable of vanquishing them ; they are powerless in the face of truth.

II

If you are assailed and tormented by certain mental images, it is important to know that you have the power to change them by focusing on them and giving them another form and colour : your will-power will end by overpowering them.

Suppose, for instance, that just before dropping off to sleep, in that twilight zone between waking and sleeping, you find yourself on a muddy road or in a dark and dangerous forest, what should you do ? Let the images continue unchallenged ? Put up with them passively ? Just before you drop off to sleep, you are on the borderline between the physical and astral worlds ; you are just about to enter the astral region, and these images bear a message : they predict something, they are a warning of unpleasant events in store for you. Or you can have the opposite experience, and find yourself in a marvellous garden, full of flowers, birds and music, and these images predict good things to come.

But let's talk about when you are the victim of sombre mental images. Even though you are beginning to slip into unconsciousness, you can still retain a certain degree of lucidity and react : you can make an effort to raise your thoughts to higher regions, where other, more luminous images will begin to take shape in your mind's eye. This does not mean that you are really going to change the course of events ; you will still have to experience trials and difficulties because, often enough, they depend on outside circumstances. But, by changing the images in your mind, you set in motion other currents and forces which will come to your rescue when difficulties do arise. You cannot prevent outside events from occurring, but you can defend yourself against them by arming yourself inwardly with the forces that will enable you to face up to them.

Winter is a difficult season, but if we have enough fuel to keep us warm we get through it all right. And the same is true of the inner life : you must be aware of what is going on within you. There is no way of avoiding the dark phantoms of the mind and the painful sensations that assail us all ; we live in a world fraught with violence of every kind and it is inevitable that we should suffer some repercussions from it. The question is not how to change the world, that is impossible, but how to improve our own, inner situation. We cannot transform the whole world but we can transform ourselves. The transformation of the world is God's business and no one will ever hold us responsible for not having done it. The one thing that is asked of us is to make up our minds to transform just one creature on earth : ourselves ; that is the only thing that we shall be held responsible for : the transformation of ourselves.

As soon as you feel the inrush of noxious currents, therefore, of gross, primitive, sensual urges, instead of letting yourself be swept away by them, in the mistaken belief that there is nothing you can do to prevent it... you must react at once. When a human being improves his inner state, the whole world is transformed because he sees it through different 'spectacles'. Why do lovers find the world so beautiful ? Because everything in them is beautiful and poetic. It may be snowing or raining, but they are together and, for them, the sun is shining, the sky is blue, the birds are singing and the flowers perfume the air : it is springtime in their hearts. Lovers are a magnificent lesson for spiritualists !

A true spiritualist has the conviction that thought is a reality and that it possesses all powers. Knowing this, he makes good use of every moment of his day to make his thought work for him ; even in the most unfavourable circumstances, when others would be unhappy, defeated or in revolt, a spiritualist manages to find light and peace, for he is above circumstances. Whereas those who don't know how to use their thought in this way, spend their time feeling sorry for themselves and are permanently defeated. They don't know that they possess an instrument capable of putting them out of the reach of circumstance and, because of their ignorance, their possibilities are always very limited and they become weaker and weaker and closer and closer to death.

Man has the power to neutralize his circumstances so that they no longer have a negative effect on him. But he has to work to achieve this. If he just waits and does nothing to improve his situation, he will be defeated by it. Even the greatest spiritual Masters, when they incarnate on this earth, have to accept appalling conditions : privations, illness and persecution. Yes, but they surmount all these difficulties because they adopt the philosophy of the spirit. So henceforth, whatever happens to you, tell yourself, 'Yes, it is true that my circumstances are very bad, but I have the power within me to trigger currents which are real and extremely powerful and which are sure to get results.' If you do this you will be on top of your circumstances ; if you don't do it is they that will always be on top of you and you will be crushed by them. If you train yourself to think like this every day, it will not be long before you find yourself vic-

torious in even the most dreadful, the most unfavourable circumstances. Yes, because you will
have been capable of setting in motion forces that
are more powerful than the circumstances.

The spirit is above everything else and when you
manage to become one with it, to identify with it,
you receive strength, peace of mind, illumination.
But how many accept this philosophy ? They do no
work with the spirit, they are always waiting for better conditions ; that is why they are so vulnerable.
If they do happen to succeed in some areas and win
a little happiness, it is only because others have
helped them or thanks to some temporary external
circumstances, not because they have the true
philosophy.

You will object, 'Yes, but what you are saying is
that we should live in the world of subjective truth.'
Exactly : I am saying that you must begin by exploring the subjective world. It is in the subjective world
that God has hidden every potentiality. Materialists
have no conscious power in the domain of thought
and feelings because they rely too much on the objective, physical, material world and have lost all
faith in the powers of the inner world. In fact, they
even try to obliterate every trace of that world.

Obviously, there is a danger here for
spiritualists : knowing that they can change the
course of their thoughts and feelings, that they can
change their sorrow into joy, their discouragement

into hope, they imagine that they can just as easily change the external world. No, that is not so ! The great advantage of the subjective world is that it puts you in touch with the invisible, subtle forces of nature. This world is a reality, but it is not a concrete material reality, and if you are so convinced that what you feel is reality that you try to convince others of it, you can expect to be bitterly disappointed. The objective and subjective worlds both exist, but in order to adjust the two realities, you have to know the correspondences and how they relate to each other. If you become totally absorbed in the inner world, the external world will cease to exist for you, and every possible anomaly, every illusion and error can follow and you will simply be grotesque. Materialists who ignore the subtle world, on the other hand, get on much better on the physical plane, but they forfeit all possibility of becoming inwardly creative.

True creators are men of thought ; creation takes place in the mind, not on the physical plane. On the physical plane one can only copy or imitate and tinker with matter. True creation takes place in the spiritual world. Even if materialists control and dominate matter and force it to work for them, they lose the kingship of the spirit : they equate themselves with matter, they sink to its level, thereby losing the power to command it ; they rob themselves of their magical power.

This is why I say that, if you become capable
of always using your will-power, your thought, your
spirit, to fashion your inner impulses, you can
become a creator, a formidable power. But don't
delude yourselves ! Even though you are capable
of making your thought obey you and of accomplishing a work of inner transformation, this
does not mean that the physical world will obey you
as well. A lot of people go off their heads because
they fail to distinguish the two worlds. I gave you
the example of lovers for whom, when they are
together, winter is turned into spring. The
springtime within them is real, but it is still winter
on the outside. If they imagine that they only have
to stretch out a hand and, abracadabra ! the birds
will sing and the snow will melt... Well, they will
have to think again ! But this is what some
spiritualists do... they imagine things ! Some even
believe that they only have to pronounce certain
magic words, like Ali Baba and the Forty Thieves,
and a rock will open up before them ; all they have
to do is say, 'Open, Sesame !' and they will find
hidden treasure and live in comfort for the rest of
their days. No, it is much more sensible to work
than to expect treasure to come to you by magic.

Of course, if a disciple continues, day after day,
to transform and embellish everything that exists
in the inner world of his own thoughts and feelings,
the currents created by this work end by influen-

cing even physical matter and he becomes capable of producing phenomena in the objective world. Yes, because everything is connected : the vibrations, particles, waves and emanations of his inner world reach out and impregnate the objective world, and the objective world can become as radiant and luminous as the subjective world. But tremendous time and practice are needed before attaining this point !

Always give priority to the spirit, therefore ; if you do this, not only will you always be above your circumstances, but your circumstances themselves will begin to change. Yes, because circumstances are inanimate, lifeless and, by working with the spirit, which is alive, you can change them. Life is never stagnant and immobile ; it is constantly changing and moving things. Use its powers of change and renewal ; get it to intervene, otherwise you will always be held up by external circumstances.

10

THE POWER
OF CONCENTRATED THOUGHT

Concentration is one of the most necessary faculties in a great many branches of activity. Engravers, surgeons and acrobats all know how important it is. They all have to concentrate in order to avoid a clumsy gesture which could be fatal. Even manual workers need to concentrate, otherwise they are liable to have an arm or a leg taken off by a machine. So many accidents happen simply because of a moment of distraction ! Concentration is the basis of all safety and all success. Generally speaking, people understand this and apply it in their professional lives, but they are a long way from realizing that it is equally important in the spiritual and psychic domains.

Many of you have probably experimented with a magnifying glass and set fire to a piece of paper by concentrating a ray of sunlight through the glass onto the paper. Why have you never thought to transpose this phenomenon onto the psychic plane ? Yes, the magnifying glass can help you to understand that if you focus your thought on one point and hold it there long enough it can set fire — symbolically speaking — to certain materials. A magnifying glass is a striking example of the power of concentration but the recent development of lasers is a far more potent example. As light has a natural tendency to spread out in all directions, the problem facing physicists was how to concentrate many light waves into one narrow beam and, once they had succeeded in doing this, they found that it could be used for all kinds of technical, medical and military purposes. Isn't the fact that physical light is all-powerful (as has been demonstrated by lasers), an additional reason to believe that spiritual light, too, is all-powerful ?

One of the best exercises in concentration that I have given you is to meditate in front of the rising sun : to focus all your powers of concentration on the sun, to the exclusion of every other thought, and remain in this sacred attitude for a long time. If you manage to do this properly, you will soon feel strengthened, enlightened and fulfilled. And if, for instance, an organ of your body is ill, you can do a great deal to make it better by directing a ray of sunlight into its cells, a ray of light, love, kindness, vitality and joy.

Yes, you can really and truly help to improve your health by mental concentration. Oh, I know : some people will think that it is a waste of time.

There are so many drugs available nowadays, you can cure anything by swallowing a pill : why bother to concentrate ? This is disastrously faulty reasoning : a passive attitude like that is no way to become stronger nor, above all, to develop the immense inner forces which will continue to serve you even after you have left this earth.

You must realize that only one thing is truly important for man, and that is his ability to concentrate on a divine reality : it is this that will enable him to continue his progress in peace for the rest of eternity. Suppose that, on leaving this world, you find yourself surrounded by an atmosphere of darkness and obscurity which prevents you from seeing either your friends or the Angels : who will come and rescue you from that solitude and darkness ? Your ability to concentrate on a divine reality. Yes, this ability endures after death because it is not the product of the brain but of the immortal spirit.

When man leaves his physical body, this ability survives in his spirit, for it is the spirit that thinks, feels and acts. It does so through the medium of the physical, material body, but you must not think that it can no longer feel, think or act when it is released from this body ; on the contrary, it is then that it can do so really powerfully. This is why a disciple who has acquired the habit of concentrating on luminous subjects, will be very powerful on the other side : he only needs to concentrate on the Lord or on light to scatter difficulties and darkness. But if he has never developed this ability during his life on earth, he will be unable to use it on the other side. This is why you must get into the habit of concentrating, every day, on the most elevated subjects.

The spirit is a tremendous power, but no one believes in this power. And do you know why ? Because they have tried it for one minute and, when they found that nothing changed, they made up their minds that they were wasting their time, that thought and the spirit were ineffectual ! The fact is, of course, that they simply have not understood. You must realize that if thought and the spirit are ineffectual, it is because matter has become so opaque, tough and leaden, that it is going to take thousands of years to change it and make it sensitive and subtle. And, as men have not even begun this work of transformation, matter still resists with all its might. If man had done some work in this direction in the past, his physical body would already be much more pliant, more accessible to the influence of thought and easier to educate. His work would have made it possible for light, the spirit, to penetrate the matter of the body. But physical realities and material conditions still predominate today, because human beings are misled by appearances and are no longer capable of seeing or feeling the world of the spirit, Heaven, the Deity.

But, to get back to the power of concentration :
we are told that there are fakirs in India who have
practised the art of concentration for so many years,
that they are capable of acting on the etheric
quintessence (known in Sanskrit as *akasha*) with
such power that they can make a seed sprout in front
of your eyes : within the space of a few hours a seed
becomes a plant which flowers and produces
delicious fruit for the delight of onlookers. This may
seem impossible, but it can quite easily be explained. The fakir influences the *akasha* in such a way
that it acts on the stereotypes contained in the seed.
Every tree stores a kind of etheric stereotype, a syn-
thesis of its special characteristics, in each of its
seeds. The shape, size and colour and all the noxious or curative properties of the parent tree,
therefore, are potentially present in its seeds but,
in the ordinary way, these characteristics will only
be actualized if the seeds are planted and watered ;
only gradually, after years of growth, nature gently brings the tree to its full stature.

However, this evolution can be hastened. Yes,
if you concentrate in such a way as to intensify the
forces of light, warmth and life from the sun, the
atmosphere and the earth, so that the seed is
nourished more rapidly than in the normal course
of nature, the growth of the plant can be greatly
accelerated. You see how simple it is : if someone
knows how to act on the akashic forces, on this

quintessence that contains all the elements that the
plant needs in order to grow (vitality, warmth, light,
magnetism and electricity), he can intensify them
and accelerate the development of the stereotypes
contained in the seed. If it is a mango seed, for instance, it only takes a few hours for the fakir to produce a tree laden with delicious fruit that everyone
can enjoy.

But the most interesting aspect of this process
is that it also exists on the spiritual plane : here too,
it is in our power to develop certain of our inherent
possibilities far more rapidly. Of course, even if we
do nothing to hasten things, our innate potential
will eventually mature, simply by the force of circumstance, but that will take millions of years : it
would be a pity to have to wait so long ! Each one
of us possesses all kinds of seeds, the germs of
various gifts, qualities and faculties that the Creator
has planted within us, but they have not yet begun
to sprout. They are still at the stage of seeds in the
ground, waiting for the warmth, water and sunlight
that will make them grow. In winter, the soil is full
of seeds of all kinds, but they cannot grow for there
is not enough light or warmth. All they can do is
wait... But as soon as spring arrives and there is a
new concentration of light and warmth, all those
seeds that have been hiding underground will start
thrusting their heads out into the light. You will,
perhaps, say, 'Everyone knows that, even children !'

Yes, everyone knows that, but when it comes to transposing phenomena of this kind onto the spiritual plane everyone is extraordinarily ignorant !

And now, if you ask me how you can find out whether those seeds, the gifts that God has planted in you, are real, I will answer : 'By exposing yourself to the sun.' It is the sun that will warm them and bring them out into the light of day. When I speak of the sun, of course, I mean, first and foremost, the spiritual sun and, only secondly, the physical sun. The sun in the physical world is there to show us how things work on the spiritual plane. But, as human beings don't believe that the spiritual sun has the power to bring out all their hidden faculties and virtues, they think that they don't need to expose themselves to its light and warmth. Is it any wonder, then, that nothing grows in their 'soil' ? They are permanently frozen and in the dark, shivering and miserable. Why don't they come closer to the spiritual Sun, the Lord, and experience the joy of seeing all their seeds sprouting and growing in their garden ?

Start today, and try to learn how to concentrate so as to set in motion potent spiritual, divine forces. It is here and now that you must begin work if you want to accomplish anything in the world of the spirit. There, as I have already explained, matter is not so dense or opaque ; on the contrary, it is pliant and docile, it submits to the commands of thought and takes on the form, dimensions and colour dictated by thought. You can do whatever you like with this subtle matter.

Well, there you are ! Consider that concentration is an extremely important exercise ; that you must practise concentrating on the most highly spiritual subjects every day. If you do so, you will feel the effects in your life very rapidly ; instead of perpetually stagnating in the same sufferings and difficulties, you will begin to grow, to free yourselves and to live lives of harmony, light and peace.

11

THE FOUNDATIONS OF MEDITATION

I

Generally speaking, meditation is not a habit that most human beings have cultivated to any great extent. From time to time, when a difficulty arises, when someone is faced with a particularly knotty problem or a very painful situation, he will become pensive and more thoughtful because he has to find a way out of his problems. But this cannot really be qualified as meditation ; it is simply an instinctive, natural response to danger or disaster. When a man finds himself in danger he instinctively reaches for help by turning his gaze inwards ; he even begins to pray, to ask for help from the Being that he had neglected when things were going well for him. He remembers that when he was a child his parents told him that this Supreme Being was all-powerful, omniscient and all-loving, so now that he has problems his instinct is to turn back to Him and, with the utmost humility in the presence of such extraordinary power, to ask Him for help. Yes, but the thing is that this only happens in extreme circumstances : in moments of danger, war, illness or death.

In the ordinary way, when people are perfectly happy and content, they have no desire to pray or meditate ; they don't think it is necessary ; they don't see the use of it. When everything is going well, people see no reason to wander off into the vague, nebulous world of meditation. It is when things go wrong, when they are unhappy or in great difficulty and they realize that concrete, material solutions are inadequate, that they turn inwards and look for help and solutions to their problems in the world above. That is all well and good, but the help they are looking for from Heaven would be far more readily forthcoming if they had not waited for a 'special occasion' before asking for it, if they had already acquired the habit of daily meditation. Without the practice of meditation it is not possible either to know oneself or to acquire self-governance or to develop spiritual qualities and virtues. In fact, if human beings have such a frail inner life and such lack of depth in their feelings and desires, it is because they fail to recognize the primordial importance of meditation.

Of course, there is no point in trying to pretend that meditation is easy : it is not. It is very difficult. As long as one is wholly absorbed in mundane occupations or a prisoner to one's own passions, meditation is impossible. Some degree of inner freedom is necessary before one's thoughts can reach up towards the Almighty. I have seen people who have meditated regularly for years, and who were wasting their time or even becoming unbalanced, because they had not realized — or did not want to realize — that certain conditions have to be fulfilled before one can meditate. It is impossible to meditate if one is not inwardly free. So many people continue with their shady deals, cheat and steal, drink and fornicate, and then they go off and 'meditate' ! Well, this is just not possible ! The nature of their activities makes meditation impossible, for it ties their thoughts down to the lower levels.

I know that it is becoming more and more fashionable to meditate nowadays, but I am afraid that this does not fill me with delight, for all I see are quantities of poor creatures rushing into something they don't understand. How can you meditate if you do not have a high ideal to free you from your moods or your licentious habits, to raise you above mere physical pleasures and appetites and lead you to Heaven ? You cannot meditate until you have overcome certain weaknesses and understood certain truths. In fact, not only can you not do so but it is even dangerous to try.

A lot of people close their eyes, strike a pose and appear to be meditating, but what is really go-

ing on inside ? The Lord only knows where they
are ! If you could see into their heads you would
probably find that they were asleep ! Is that
meditation ? You can even go and see public demonstrations of meditation ! It is perfectly ri-
diculous. How can anyone possibly meditate in
public ? Or if he could, it would mean that he
was so advanced, so free of all ties, that he was
capable of meditating anywhere and at any time
because his spirit was ceaselessly in communication with the divine world. But this kind of
love for the sublime world above supposes a very
exceptional level of evolution which is not the case
of those who give public demonstrations of how to
meditate !

If you want an accurate idea of how most people
meditate, look at a cat : a cat can sit for hours in
front of a mouse-hole, meditating on how to catch
a mouse ! Well, that is what most human beings
do : they meditate about how to catch a two-legged
'mouse' !

Meditation is not quite so simple as many people
think. You have to be very advanced to meditate
and, above all, you must have an immense love of
the divine world. If this is the case, then your
thoughts are already focused, and you can begin to
meditate without any special effort, almost in spite
of yourself : your mind is so free that it sets out
on its own, as it were, to do its work.

People have sometimes said to me, 'I've been trying to meditate for years, but my brain always seems to get stuck and I never get anywhere.' Why is this ? The reason is that they have not understood that the different moments of one's life are not disconnected and cut off from each other in water-tight compartments. Each moment is connected to all those that have gone before and which we lump together and call 'the past'. They don't realize that their past can weigh them down and hinder them and, as they are sincerely anxious to meditate, they insist and do violence to their brain with the result that it seizes up and refuses to function. It never seems to occur to them that if they want to meditate, they are going to have to get not only their brain but their whole organism ready for this sort of work. In other words they are going to have to tidy up their lives. Suppose you have been quarrelling with someone : the next morning, when you are trying to meditate, the whole scene comes back to you and you go over the quarrel in your mind, remembering all the insults you gave and received and planning what you will say to him when you meet again. So much for your meditation ! Instead of flying up into divine regions, you will have spent your time going over and over the past, unable to shut out the endless stream of people and events that comes crowding into your mind.

And the same thing repeats itself year after year :
no wonder your meditations don't seem to get
any results.

Man is capable of becoming all-powerful, but
only if he knows a certain number of truths and,
in particular, the truth that every moment of our
lives is connected to all those that have gone before.
This is what Jesus meant when he said that we
should not worry about the morrow. Yes, because
if you live as you should today, the morrow will
find you free : you will be in a position to dispose
of yourself at will and concentrate your thoughts
on whatever you please, because yesterday's affairs
are all in order. Whereas, if you live a disordered
life, every day will find you hobbled by the loose
ends of the day before, and you will have to race
about in all directions trying to set things straight
and remedy your past mistakes, instead of being free
to work in the present and create the future.

An enlightened disciple who wants to meditate,
therefore, prepares himself in advance by purify-
ing himself and disengaging himself from all kinds
of useless preoccupations. He tries to develop to the
highest possible degree his desire to improve and
perfect himself in order to help others and be an
example, a model, a true son of God. In accordance
with Jesus' instructions to his disciples, he is
animated by the sublime desire to do the will of God

in everything. But wishing and wanting alone will not enable us to carry out the precepts Jesus gave us : we also need a certain amount of knowledge. A great many people want to live according to these precepts but without success, because they do not know how to set about it. If you have left the hot-water tap running or the gas turned on, or forgotten the baby in the bath, it will come back to you in a flash just as you are about to meditate — and that will be the end of your meditation !

Prepare yourself in advance, therefore, and when you are free in body, mind and feelings, when you have finally escaped from the prison of your everyday life, you can begin to rise within yourself. You can begin to feel that other life, a life that is so new, vast, broad and deep that you feel yourself expanding in it and drawn out of yourself into another, higher region. And this higher region, in reality, is within you. Yes, this divine life flows within you, and in experiencing it you experience a few moments of true life. In this way the divine world begins to awaken within you, and once this has happened, you can never forget it ; henceforth you have the conviction that the soul is a reality, that the divine world exists and that countless creatures inhabit it. Why this firm conviction ? Because you have managed to set in motion forces that were previously unknown to you, forces that are tremendously powerful and beneficial whereas, before this, you were in the grip of hostile, corrosive forces which were gradually destroying you.

This has always been known and taught by Initiates. Meditation is a psychological and philosophical question ; it is an act of cosmic dimensions of the greatest importance. Once a disciple has tasted the sweetness of this higher world his convictions are strengthened and he can feel that his faculties begin to obey him. When he wants to set his mind to work it obeys him, and when he wants it to stop it stops ; it is as though the cells of his whole being had decided to conform. If he has not reached this mastery it will take him hours and hours to find inner peace and quiet because his cells continue their restless movement and refuse to listen to him. They say : 'If you think you can scare us you're making a big mistake ! We can't take you seriously and we're certainly not afraid of you. We have no respect for you because you have shown how stupid and ignorant you are !' and they go on doing exactly as they please. You all know what I am talking about, don't you ? And then, on other days, you find that your cells obey you because, knowingly or unknowingly, you have reached a higher level and released higher forces and, in doing so, have gained greater authority over your cells which recognize a hierarchical authority and are ready to obey their master.

After all, isn't this true in every area of life ?

In businesses and government or in the armed forces, every individual strives to move up the hierarchical ladder and become manager, chairman of the board, chief of staff or general, because when he reaches the top and, especially, when he sports all his ribbons and medals, he knows that others will respect and obey him. Even if a man is a complete idiot or a tyrant it makes no difference : it is his rank that commands obedience. And where do you suppose that this sense of hierarchy comes from ? It is not a human invention, for human beings invent nothing. Through intuition, instinct or trial and error, they simply discover what already exists in nature, and hierarchy is something that exists throughout nature. In the heavens (stars and constellations), on earth (rivers, mountains, trees and animals) and even in man, everything is ordered hierarchically.

And since this is so, since it is common knowledge that someone who wants to be a leader and impose his will on others has to be at least one step above them, why should it be difficult to understand that in spiritual things too, we have to be a step above our own inhabitants if we want them to obey us ? The principle and the practical applications are the same on all levels. And this is precisely the aim of an Initiate : to win the obedience of his own inner world. He is not interested in being obeyed by mountains, stars, animals or men ; he is only interested in achieving self-dominance, in being the master of his own physical body, of his own thoughts and feelings, and he works constantly to this end.

Spiritual exercises such as meditation enable man to free himself progressively from these fetters, this prison, the chains that keep him in perpetual bondage to the subterranean world. So many have been caught and held captive ! Lacking the light, they let themselves sink lower and lower, deep into this fearful world. Call it Hell, call it the Devil, it makes no difference ; it is a very real world in which many are inextricably lost, simply because they did not choose to use the means of salvation taught by Initiatic Science. They thought they were being very intelligent whereas, in fact, they were simply being stubborn and proud — and look where they are now !

The only way to escape from torment and anguish is to meditate. But, as I have already said, in order to meditate one first has to settle a certain number of questions. When the mother of a large family wants to make a cake, for instance, she waits until the children are in bed and asleep before she begins ; she cannot get anything done while they are all round her, clinging onto her skirts and clamouring for attention. And we have to do the same : we have this large family within us, all those noisy, high-spirited children, and we must make them keep quiet so as to be free to do our work, and then, once it is done, we can go back to them and share out the cake !

If you want to meditate you have to understand the nature of psychic work. You must never try to rush the brain, for example, and force it to concentrate from one moment to the next, for this does violence to the cells of the nervous system, and the result is that they seize up and you get a headache ! The first thing to do is to relax, to remain passive, as it were, while at the same time keeping an eye on the gradual pacification of your cells. Naturally, it takes practice to be able to do this quite quickly, but eventually you will find that it only takes a few moments. To begin with, therefore, you must use gentleness, peace and love and, above all, avoid any form of violence. This is the secret of a good meditation. And once you feel that your nervous system is well disposed and that your 'batteries' have been recharged (for this passive attitude gives the body an opportunity to replenish its supplies of energy), then you can focus your thoughts on the topic of your choice.

If you want to do your work every day without tiring ; if you want to be active, dynamic, ready and willing to undertake important work every day, you must learn how to use your brain correctly. This is very important. From now on, therefore, if you

want to keep up your spiritual activities for a long
time, you must be very careful about this : never
rush at a subject of meditation all at once. Even
if it is something very dear to your heart, a subject
you are very attached to, don't dash at it, otherwise there will be a violent reaction. Begin work
quietly and gently, therefore. Immerse yourself in
the ocean of cosmic harmony and draw strength
from it, and when you feel that your energies have
been renewed, you can go ahead with your spiritual
work and put your whole being into it. Yes, the intellect is not the only faculty concerned when it
comes to spiritual work : your whole body, every
single cell of your body, should be involved.

During the first few minutes, therefore, try not
to think. Simply glance into yourself to see that
everything is functioning smoothly and pay attention, only, to your breathing. Breathe regularly,
don't think, allow yourself simply to feel, to be
aware that you are breathing. You will notice that
your regular breathing induces a harmonious
rhythm in your thoughts and feelings and in your
whole body, and this is very beneficial.

Some of you may say : 'As far as I'm concerned,
I don't know what meditation is and I don't want
to know. I'm willing to make sacrifices ; I'm ready
to be charitable and do good to others, and that's
enough !' No, that is not enough, for our actions

can transgress certain laws, complicate things and even be very destructive if we do not begin by meditating. Why should we meditate ? Because only meditation clears our vision and allows us to see reality as it is, to see whom to help, how and when to help them, and so on.

You can meditate on all kinds of subjects : health, beauty, wealth, intelligence, power, glory, the Angels, the Archangels and the Heavenly Hierarchies. All of these subjects are good, but the best of all is to meditate on God Himself in order to be steeped in His love, light and strength, in order to live for a brief moment in His eternity... and always meditate in order to serve God, to do His will and be one with Him. No meditation is more beneficial or more powerful than this. Any other kind of meditation is motivated by some form of self-interest : hopes of financial advantage, the will to use occult forces for personal enrichment or to gain power over others. Initiates understand that what is most advantageous for them is, precisely, not to seek their own personal advantage, but to seek to become servants of God. All the rest is tainted with black magic and witchcraft. And this means that, without realizing it, most occultists dabble in witchcraft because they use these invisible forces to gain wealth and power or to enthrall women, not for the service of God. So, you see, there are many different shades and degrees of meditation !

Obviously, one has to begin by meditating on subjects that are not too remote or difficult. Human beings are made in such a way that it is not natural to them to exist in an abstract environment. They need to hang on to things that are visible and tangible, to things that are close to them and that they love. It is very easy, for instance, to concentrate on food when one has not eaten for a long time. It takes no special effort to be like that cat we were talking about, which concentrated so hard on the mouse ! We don't need to try : it just happens, all by itself. And think of how a young man concentrates on the girl he loves : for hours and even days on end, simply because he loves her. And here, too, there is no need for any special effort, but what a meditation ! He can't tear himself away !

So begin by meditating on something that gives you pleasure, something you enjoy. Later, you can go on to other things, but begin with something you really like, something that attracts you (of course it must be something spiritual, not just anything). In this way, by beginning with subjects that are already congenial to you, you will develop your own means and methods of work and, later on, you can leave these subjects and fly higher, to more distant, more abstract regions. It is obvious that if you begin by trying to meditate on space, time and eternity, you will not get very far ! Later on, you will be capable of fixing your thoughts on such things as the void, the depths of nothingness and so on, but begin with something easier and then, gradually, you will get to these more abstract subjects.

However, I must repeat what I said earlier : the most sublime meditation is to be in communion with God, to submit to Him, to want to serve Him and be nothing more than an instrument in His hands. When you melt into the Lord in this way, all the divine qualities, all His power, love and wisdom, all His immensity floods into you and, one day, you will become a divinity. When they hear this, some people will object : 'What pride to think that you can become a divinity !' And to that I can only reply, 'Read the Gospels. Didn't Jesus say "Be ye perfect as your heavenly Father is perfect" ?' There is no ideal higher than this and it was Jesus himself who gave it to us, but Christians have forgotten that. A great many of them think that it is sufficient to go and light a candle in church, from time to time and, for the rest, to look after one's own little chicken-run in order to be good Christians. What an idea ! As though the Kingdom of God would ever be any nearer if everybody behaved like that ! Oh, those poor Christians, they adhere strictly to the principle that one must not ask too much of human beings for fear of falling into the sin of pride ! Well, what I am telling you is exactly the opposite : we must harbour the highest possible ideal in our hearts, souls and spirits, the high ideal

of becoming a totally compliant instrument in the
hands of God, so that God Himself may think, feel
and act through us. If this is your ideal you will be
abandoning yourself to the will of Wisdom and
Light, you will be putting yourself totally at the service of omniscient Light so that it may guide you
in all your ways.

But man is also on earth and what is he here
for ? Jesus said (You see, I always refer to what
Jesus said, for he said it all ! What would be the
point of inventing anything else ?). So, Jesus said :
'Thy will be done on earth as it is in Heaven.' 'On
earth as in Heaven' means that the earth must reflect
Heaven. And the 'earth' is our own, personal earth,
the earth of our physical body. And this means that
once we have worked to reach the summit we must
then bring the summit down into the organization
of our physical body. Immortality is on high, light
is on high, harmony, peace, beauty and all subtle
realities are on high. And everything that exists on
high must be brought down and be incarnate here
below, on the physical level. Ask to become a servant of God, therefore, and, at the same time, work
at the formation of that other body within you that
we call the Body of Light, the Body of Glory, the
Immortal Body, the Body of Christ. The Gospels
speak of this body, too, but Christians have never
paid much attention to it. The truth of the matter
is that they are not really interested in understanding

the Gospels in depth : they are anything but real Christians !

You will, perhaps, say that to want to tend the earth is not a very glorious ideal, whereas Hindus... Yes, I know : Hindus and Buddhists are only interested in escaping from this earth of sorrow, suffering and strife. That is their philosophy, but it is not the philosophy of Christ. Christ's philosophy is to bring Heaven down to earth, to bring about the Kingdom of God and His Righteousness on earth. This is the Kingdom that Jesus was working for, and he asked his disciples to work for it also. So that is what we have to do : work for the coming of the Kingdom of God on earth and, to begin with, in our own physical bodies. This is the true philosophy. I am not interested in what others may have understood.

'Thy will be done on earth as it is in Heaven.' Yes, but where are the labourers for this work ? Men have other philosophies in their heads, and this means that they will have to keep coming back to earth until they manage to turn it into a Garden of Eden. When they have done this, they will go to another planet, leaving the earth to the animals, which also have to evolve. This surprises you, doesn't it ? You see, men have been sent to earth to work as labourers on a building site, but they are not interested in their work ; they are only interested in having a good time. You must not neglect

your duty in that way : every day you must work
to transform the earth into a Paradise. If you do
this the Lord will commend you, saying : 'Well
done. You have been good and faithful servants and
worked well in my fields. Now it is time for you
to enter into the Joy and Glory of My Kingdom.'
In the Gospels, too, Jesus speaks of labourers who
are sent out to work in the fields. Well, it is we who
are those labourers. And where are the fields in
which we are working ? And what have we
planted ?

You are certainly familiar, also, with the par-
able of the talents. The idea is the same. The un-
profitable servant who was punished because he
had buried his talents represents all those who
don't work, who are only interested in making
money, having a good time and making the earth
a more comfortable place for themselves. This
has nothing to do with Christ's philosophy. We
have been sent to earth with a specific task, and
when we have done it, the Lord will give us all
the rest ; the whole universe will be ours. This is
why it saddens me to see the conception that so
many occultists and so many spiritual and mys-
tical people have of life on this earth. They marry and have children, eat and drink and make
merry exactly like the most ignorant of men.
What are they doing about the work for which they
have been sent to earth ? Exactly nothing ! And

this applies to you, too : take a close look into yourselves and you will see that what you do bears no relation to Christ's philosophy.

There ! What I have given you today are the two best subjects for meditation : how to devote yourselves entirely to the service of the Godhead, and how to go about bringing Heaven down to earth as a concrete, physical reality. The whole meaning of life is contained in these two activities. All other activities have a certain significance, of course, but no other activity has this divine significance. God has created man in his own image ; He has created man so that he shall come to resemble Him. And if you don't believe this, go and ask Him ! All my life I have sought the very best, and I have found it. But to have found it is no reason to sit back and twiddle your thumbs. Quite the contrary : now is the time to set to work, because that which has been 'found' must now be translated into concrete reality here, on earth, just as it already exists in Heaven. The fact that many things do already exist here, on earth, on the mental level, is not sufficient. They must also be made to exist on the physical level, and it is this that is long and difficult.

There is a great deal more that could be said about this, but that is enough for today. It is essential that you understand the importance of meditation and, above all, that you understand that, if your meditations are to bear fruit, you must watch over your thoughts, feelings and actions, in other words, over your whole way of life. Begin by meditating on simple, easy subjects and, gradually, you can go on to more sublime things and, one day, all your work will be focused on becoming an instrument in the hands of God in order to establish His Kingdom on earth. There is nothing more divine or more glorious than this. This is the perfect fulfilment of divine law, the perfection of wisdom.

Never forget that it is by your meditations that you allow your inner Self to express itself and reach its full flowering. This is the means by which you can release this mysterious, subtle being so that it can gaze on all that exists in infinite space and then reproduce it on the physical plane. Of course, we are practically never conscious of the realities that this being gazes on, but if we continue to do these exercises regularly and often, little by little they will reach our consciousness and constitute an inner treasure that will always be with us.

You must learn to enjoy meditation. Meditation must become a need in you, in your minds, hearts and wills. It must become a pleasure without which life is insipid and meaningless. You should look forward impatiently to those moments when you can, at last, immerse yourself in Eternity and drink the Elixir of Immortal Life, and I see no sign of this joyful impatience in you ! You should be like a drunkard who thinks of nothing but his wine and, when the time comes for your meditation, your reaction should be : 'At last ! My soul, my spirit, my heart are free to embrace the whole universe for a few moments. Free to come face to face with Immensity !'

II

The Lord has given every single one of His creatures the possibility of finding the food best suited to it. Look at the animals : there are countless different species of insects, fish, fowl and mammals, and nature provides a different kind of food that is specially prepared for every single one of them. How is it, then, that man is the only species that does not find what it needs ? As far as physical nourishment is concerned, of course, human beings know what to look for and how to get it, but where their spiritual, psychic nourishment is concerned, they have no idea what they need or how to find it. And yet, this too, is available in abundance throughout the universe, we only need to know what region we must go to, to find what we are looking for.

Of course, if you start exploring a swampy region infested with mosquitoes, wasps and snakes, that is what you will find. And if it is eagles you are looking for, you will have to go up into the mountains. Suppose you feel the need to contemplate the beauty of nature, but you live in an attic : you will have to go out for a walk in a forest or a garden or along the seashore. If you want learning, you will have to go to a university or a library. In other words, we have to find the region that corresponds to whatever it is we are looking for. But if this is true on the physical level, it is equally true on the spiritual level, and this is why the disciples in an Initiatic school dedicate a certain period every day to the work of meditation. Their meditation takes them to the different regions of the invisible world where they know that they can find what they need to remain on an even keel and grow spiritually.

You will ask : 'But how can we find the right regions ? Who can show us the way to them ? At least on the physical level there are geography books, maps, atlases and encyclopaedias that give us all the information we need. But how can one find one's way in the invisible world ?' Ah, that is the great question. And the answer is that on the psychic plane there is a phenomenon analogous to that which enables a diviner to use a 'clue' to find someone who is lost. The clue can be a lock of his hair or an object that he has handled, for divination is based on the law of affinity and, in the spiritual domain, it is your thoughts that are the 'clue' which reach out into space and make contact with elements with which they have an affinity. The spiritual world is organized in such a way that the mere fact of thinking about a particular person, element or region has the effect of putting one in direct contact with the objects of one's thought, wherever they may be be. So, unlike the physical world, for which we need maps and precise directions, in the spiritual world it is not necessary to know exactly where those we wish to contact may be.

On the spiritual, divine plane of being, it is not necessary to go to great lengths to find something ; all we need to do is to concentrate our powers of thought with great intensity and they will take us wherever we want to be. If you think about health, you are immediately in the realm of health ; if you think about love, you are in the realm of love ; if you think about music, you are in the realm of music ; in fact, if you are particularly sensitive and have a gift for it, you may even perceive an echo of that Heavenly music. For you must not think that the great composers actually 'invented' the music they wrote. No, they transcribed what they heard on high and, in fact, they were often incapable of transcribing exactly what they heard, for no earthly notes or harmonies are capable of really reproducing the music of the heavenly regions. Painters and poets and all artists have the same problem, for man is not yet capable of receiving and transmitting all the beauty of the divine world. He is not ready yet, but he will be ready, one day, if he undertakes the serious spiritual work of replacing all his old, tarnished, worn-out particles with pure, heavenly, bright, new particles.

You will ask, 'But where can we find those heavenly particles ?' As I have just explained, if you think about them your thoughts will find them for you. You only have to think about these bright new particles and imagine them in all their subtle, shining purity and they will be drawn to you and automatically push out the others and take their place. Of course, this will not happen all at once ; it depends on the intensity of your love and faith and on how hard you work, but one day all the particles within you that were out of harmony with the heavenly regions will be replaced, and you will be capable of perceiving and grasping the subtlest and most sublime realities of the universe.

Ever since scientists discovered that the universe was full of sound waves, they have been building increasingly sensitive instruments with which to receive and decode them. But what the scientists do not know is that these instruments have always existed in man. Yes, for the Creator, who has designed man for a future of indescribable magnificence, has provided him with instruments and sensitive antennae capable of receiving and transmitting all the intelligence and splendour of His Creation. If, for the moment, man is unable to do any of this, it is because he has never worked along these lines, he never practises ; in fact he is not even aware that he has all these possibilities within him. But he has, they do exist : he has all the instruments he needs and they are only waiting to be set in motion. These instruments are what we call the *chakras* and also certain centres in the brain, the nervous system and the solar plexus. But, at the moment, all these highly sensitive instruments are asleep and men are incapable of receiving and understanding the signals which are constantly arriving from every corner of the universe, even from the most distant constellations. As a matter of fact, this is just as well, because there are so many of them that in man's present stage of development, anyone who did receive them would be driven out of his mind or struck dead. But they will no longer be dangerous once man has developed sufficient inner strength to stand up to their power.

If we illustrate this with a comparison perhaps it will make it clearer : I suppose you have all seen how a pumpkin or melon grows, hanging from a stem that is so slender that it can easily be broken when the fruit is small, but as the fruit swells and gets heavier and heavier the stem gets stronger and stronger, and by the time the fruit is ripe it is capable of carrying a very heavy load. Well, the same thing happens with human beings. Progressively, as a person meditates regularly and begins to receive cosmic waves, something grows and develops within him which enables him to stand up to greater and greater tension. The important thing is that this must be done gradually. People who want to learn everything in a rush and develop all their faculties at once are bound to end by being unbalanced. They are like the patient who was given some medicine by his doctor and told to take ten drops every day for a month. 'A whole month ?' said he ; 'That's much too long !' and swallowed it all in one go... and dropped dead ! No ! You must learn to work with patience and regularity and, in this way, your organism will have a chance to grow gradually stronger and be better able to withstand great strain.

So here you have the essence of what you need to know : through meditation you have the power to be in touch with and receive all the elements of the universe that you need. By means of the law of affinities, it is your thoughts that go and seek out these elements. In fact, it is the same thing with human beings : when you want to think about somebody, even though there are five billion people in the world, your thought goes directly to the one person you want to think about and to no one else. It is as though your thought had been magnetized and was drawn to exactly the right person.

From now on, therefore, if you want to obtain a particular element from the universe or if you want to contact a particular entity, don't trouble yourself about their whereabouts ; just think of them and your thought will fly straight to them. You could make the comparison, if you like, with the way in which a specially trained police dog can smell out somebody if it has sniffed a piece of clothing or a handkerchief belonging to him. A person's emanations are extremely subtle, but they impregnate his belongings, and the dog's sense of smell is so keen that it can follow the scent for miles and pick out the right person infallibly from amongst hundreds. This is what our thoughts do when we send them out into space to find not only elements, but also visible or invisible entities which can strengthen, enlighten and help us.

12

CREATIVE PRAYER

I

Even if you were ground to dust so fine that you think there could be nothing left of you, there would always be one atom left, one atom which can never be destroyed and with which you are capable of rebuilding the whole universe. And that atom is the gift of prayer and supplication. This is the greatest of God's gifts to men ; without it the human race would have disappeared long ago.

No one has ever heard of this 'atom of prayer' ; in fact, you may find the notion totally unacceptable and impossible to take seriously. And yet you have already learned, in Initiatic Science, of the existence of a very special atom, situated at the tip of a man's heart, which records everything that he thinks, feels and experiences in the course of his life. It does not have the power to intervene or change anything ; all it does is record events. Actually, it is a minute spool which unwinds continuously from the moment a person is born until he dies ; and when he dies it stops unwinding and is detached from him.

Well, there is also this other atom in man which has the power to ask for the help it needs to remedy a situation. If this atom is not developed, because its owner never prays, then his life will unfold strictly along the lines predetermined by destiny. To be sure, the atom of prayer cannot change the general outline of a person's life, it is extremely difficult to modify that, but it can change certain things on the subtle, etheric plane. This is why people who are in the habit of praying suffer less than others. When difficulties arise, they are less subject to inner discouragement, bitterness or desolation. Many distressing events (war, for instance), often depend on the human collectivity ; no one can avoid them. In wartime it is impossible not to be affected by privations and misfortune, but someone who prays, who is active in his soul and spirit, transforms these difficulties inwardly. Outwardly, events are the same for all, but in circumstances which defeat and discourage others — or even drive them to suicide — he will find the strength, nourishment and encouragement he needs.

You must not simply endure suffering ; you must not just resign yourselves and allow yourselves to be victimized ; you must try to remedy the situation. You will not be able to improve everything ; you are not strong enough for that yet, but the little you can do is like a seed that is already beginning to bear fruit. If you were destined to be 100%

in the cold and dark, perhaps you will manage to be only 99% in the cold and dark ! You pronounce a few words, say a prayer, concentrate on a luminous image, and each of these actions is a cry for help. Why don't you observe what goes on in life ? I am always telling you that that is where you should find your lessons. See how a child behaves : who told it that a word, a cry was something power-ful ? When it is in danger, it screams 'Mummy !' Who taught it to use that magic word ? If her child did not call out, its mother would never know that it was in danger but, as soon as she hears the scream, she rushes to the rescue ! Why don't human beings do at least as much as a little child, and cry out for help from Heaven ?

Nowadays, people are gradually losing the habit of prayer, and it is a great pity. People say, 'What's the point of praying when we have everything we need ?' But the fact is that prayer belongs to a dif-ferent dimension. Even if you have everything you need, you must still pray. Why ? Because prayer is a creation. That surprises you, doesn't it ? Every creature needs to create ; but if you have not developed certain faculties, if you have never cultivated intelligence and light, you cannot really create : the best you can do is copy, reproduce things. It is the same for a man and woman, who have never done any inner spiritual work before con-ceiving a child : they can only reproduce their own physical and moral weaknesses in their children. They think that they are creating, but the truth is that they are simply reproducing themselves. True creation exists on a much higher level, and if a man who wants to create knows this, he will realize that he must surpass and transcend himself so that his soul and spirit may receive elements from the heavenly regions. When he does this, whatever he produces will always contain elements which are superior to the common run, because he has succeeded in reaching out to Heaven, in pulling himself up and drawing down something from a great height.

True prayer is a creation. When you pray you are not simply asking for help from the boss or the chairman of the board because he is in a position to give you something, or applying to your bank manager for a loan ; you are not simply begging for a friendly glance from a woman. No, you will never gain much from that kind of prayer, because the people you are praying to are on the same level and have the same failings as yourself.

True prayer creates a link with the most sublime of all Beings, the Creator of Heaven and earth. When we pray to this sublime Being we are creating a bond with Him, with His immensity, His infinity, and thanks to this bond we can make contact with and capture elements of the higher worlds and bring them back into our everyday world, for the benefit of all creatures. For this is something that you must realize : the elements, particles and 'electrons' of this sublime region are so powerful that, even if you manage to capture only one, it will work unimaginable transformations ! You will feel it vibrating within you as it purifies, enlightens and heals you and restores harmony to your whole being ; and this beneficial, radiant state of harmony will influence all those you come in contact with, and they, too, will begin to be transformed.

Even the weakest, most destitute of human beings possesses this atom of prayer and has the power to work with it. Even if someone lacks money, food and clothing, even if he is in prison, he can be very powerful. Talents, money and strength are not given to all, but all can use the power of this atom to ask, to insist that the luminous spirits on high come and help them. If you don't ask for help when you have to face up to great difficulties, you will be powerless to do anything about them. This atom of prayer is the only thing that can remedy every situation, but you must give it some work to do, otherwise you will simply have to put up with whatever was planned for you. The power of this atom is in the psychic dimension, that is to say, in the area of your thoughts and emotions. When you pray, even if nothing changes in your external circumstances, you cannot remain unchanged. If there is a war, it will continue ; if it is freezing you will be cold ; if it rains, you will get wet ; yes, but your prayer will have changed something inside you.

A man may be dying all alone, abandoned and destitute and yet, thanks to prayer, he can die joyfully, in peace and light, whereas, in the same conditions, someone who does not pray will be devoured by sentiments of revolt and hatred. Even if there is nothing one can do to change one's external circumstances, prayer is enormously effective, if only for one's next incarnation. Most people do not know why religion has always tried to convince criminals or unbelievers to repent and ask for God's forgiveness before dying. It is because of the importance of that final moment. If someone who has been a believer and led a good, virtuous life rebels against God or loses his faith at the last moment, he destroys all the good he did during his lifetime. Yes, because it is the last moment that counts.

So you can see how important it is to know the laws and to abide by them. If you have not managed to change anything in this life, it is not of absolute importance ; as long as you live the last moments of your life in the right disposition, your future destiny will be changed, your next incarnation will be better than this one. Never forget this.

II

Jesus said, 'When you pray, go into your room, and when you have shut your door, pray to your Father who is in the secret place.' What is this secret place that Jesus was talking about ? Simply an inner state of consciousness. Whenever a disciple manages to create conditions of silence and peace within himself, whenever he feels the inner need to express his love to the Lord, he is in that secret place. Perhaps you are wondering where this secret place is : it can be in your heart, your mind or your soul. You are in this secret place when you manage to gain access to a state of higher consciousness.

Suppose, for instance, that you are meditating on a sublime reality that is really beyond your power to grasp and then, after a little while, you begin to understand. What has happened ? Where did that understanding come from ? It came from your own spirit which has always possessed it from all eternity, but it was a domain to which your consciousness had not previously had access. For man does not know what goes on in his subconscious, but nor does he know what goes on on high, in heaven, in his own heaven, his spirit, his superconsciousness.

You can shut yourself up between the four walls of your room to pray, but if you don't love the Lord, if you cannot reach that state of fervour which constitutes prayer, you will never reach nor enter into the secret place. For the secret place is that state of intense concentration, of peace and inner silence, in which everything else is extinguished, in which the only thing that moves is your prayer, the inner word that travels through space. When you are in this state, whether you know it or not, you are in the secret place.

The secret place is a magnificent and very profound symbol which was certainly known long before Jesus. Every Initiate knows that, in order to pray, one has to enter this place ; if your prayer does not come from there, Heaven cannot hear it. Why not ? Well, it is as though you were out in the street and you wanted to talk to a friend in another town : you cannot do so unless you go into a telephone booth, because that is where you will find an instrument that can put you in touch with your friend. If you stayed outside in the street, you could shout for all you're worth, but your friend would not hear you. Similarly, if you want Heaven to hear you, you must go into that secret place that Jesus talked about, for it is equipped with 'telephones' by means of which you can communicate with the higher worlds. Also, when you go into a telephone booth in a busy street, you close the door, because you need silence in order to hear and be heard. And this is why you also need silence in this secret place : you cannot do any inner work in the midst of noise.

It is important, therefore, to understand that you have a secret, silent place within you and that you must go in and shut the door behind you. To shut the door means not to let all kinds of other thoughts and desires in with you, otherwise they will interfere with your communication with Heaven and you will not get an answer. It is only if you are in this secret chamber that your call can go through correctly : you speak and you can hear, you ask Heaven for something and you get an answer. If the answer Heaven gives you does not come through clearly, it is because you have forgotten to close the door. The secret place, therefore, is a hidden, silent room. You must not let anyone else hear what you say or whom you are talking to. Naturally, you cannot always prevent someone from seeing that you are praying, but the less they see the better. The Gospels tell us of the Pharisee who went up to the Temple in Jerusalem and prayed with ostentation ! That is exactly the opposite of the secret place.

One could say that this secret room is the heart, the silence of the heart. Not, of course, the heart that corresponds to the astral plane, the site of all

our ignoble desires and lusts, but the spiritual heart :
the soul. As long as one has not managed to attain
true silence, it means that one has not yet reached
this room. There are so many 'rooms' in man and
very few human beings have ever discovered which
one, of all these rooms, is the one that loves silence.
Most people have strayed into other rooms and try
to pray there, but as these other rooms are not
equipped with the proper instruments, Heaven cannot hear their thoughts and prayers. If you want
your prayer to be heard, you have to comply with
certain conditions.

Why, for example, did the Initiates of the past
teach people to join their hands when they prayed ?
It is a symbolic gesture : true prayer is a question
of joining the two principles : heart and intellect.
If your heart is alone in what it asks for, if your
intellect stands aside and refuses to join in, your
prayer will not be heard. If you want it to be heard,
it must stem from both the heart and the intellect,
from both thought and feelings, that is to say, from
the two principles, masculine and feminine. In-
numerable paintings show people in prayer, even
children, with their hands joined, but no one has
ever understood the profound significance of this
gesture. Of course, this does not mean that one must
necessarily join one's hands physically when one
prays. It is not the physical gesture that is important ; what is important is one's inner attitude. We

have to join the soul and the spirit, the heart and the intellect, for it is their union that gives prayer its power and makes it the projection of something truly potent : you give and receive at the same time, you are both active and receptive.

People still have a great many misconceptions about prayer. They imagine that what counts are the words they use. No, very often your words fall short of the mark, they never manage to get up to Heaven. A man's mouth may murmur words, but he is not really praying if nothing vibrates within him. To be sure, the words you say are very important for the realization of your prayer, but only if your desire and your thought are already powerful on the spiritual plane ; if this is the case, then the words are like a signature which allows the forces on high to be set in motion.

Suppose that you want to awaken sentiments of love for God in yourself : as feelings are a purely psychic reality, you do not need to use words ; you can achieve this simply through the strength of your desire. But if you want to obtain something on the physical, material plane, then the spoken word is necessary. But, in spite of this, it is the intensity of your thought and feeling that are the essence of prayer for, without that, you could recite words for hours on end but you would not get any results ; your prayer would not be answered. As a matter of fact, you can feel it yourself when your prayer

has been heard. There are days when you experience
such a sense of strength and fulfilment that you
know that Heaven has heard you, at last. This does
not mean that you can expect immediate results on
the physical plane. No, the realization will not be
immediate, but your prayer has been heard, your
request has been noted, and that is what counts :
to know that you have been heard !

Everything depends on the intensity of your
prayer, therefore, and this intensity always depends
on your ability to disengage your thoughts and feelings from all extraneous preoccupations. This is why
your attitude is so important : you must feel yourself
to be totally free of other involvements. For an hour
or two, leave everything else to one side, and immerse yourself in intense spiritual work, for that is
the only way for your prayer to be answered.

As there is a correspondence between the subtle world of thought, feeling and energy, and the
world of matter, every time you manage to rise to
a higher level of consciousness, it attracts very pure
materials from the cosmos which you can use to
build a body of light, a body of glory. You must
begin by working on the spiritual plane ; the
material plane will automatically follow on from
there and transform itself.

Everything spiritual has a material correspondence ; every particle of matter has its correspondence on the spiritual plane. You only have

to work on the spiritual plane by means of your thought and prayer, for it is these invisible currents that attract elements from the sublime regions on high. Initiates have always based their work on this law of correspondences, and if they have such total trust in divine Wisdom, it is because they know that what is divine within will be divine without. Their only concern is to make sure that what they themselves do is right and harmonious. For the rest, they know that the laws of nature are faithful and that whatever is accomplished on the spiritual plane will, one day, be accomplished on the physical plane.

13

REACHING FOR THE UNATTAINABLE

The search for God is long and very demanding, to be sure. Sometimes one feels very disappointed, one has the impression that one is working in a vacuum. But this is only an impression. One is like a man who is digging for water : he cannot see it yet, but he carries the idea of water in his mind and in his heart and soul. He lives with the thought, the idea, the hope of finding water. And even if that water has not begun to flow physically, it is already flowing in him. In the same way, although he who seeks God may seem to find nothing at all, he is working with an extremely powerful reality that is living within him. He can say, 'To be sure, I haven't found God yet, but He is reflected in my thoughts and feelings ; my hope and faith are God.'

Or take the example of two men, a gold prospector and an alchemist : day after day, the gold prospector sifts through the sands of a river, gradually getting rich as he collects grain after grain of gold dust. In the meantime the alchemist is searching for the Philosophers' Stone which will transform metals into gold and, for a long time, he finds nothing and continues to be poor. But if, after years or even centuries of labour, he finally finds the Stone (and if he works according to the rules, he is bound to find it), he will immediately be the richest man in the world : he will be able to change whole mountains into gold !

He who seeks God is like the alchemist who has not yet found the Philosophers' Stone and, at the same time, he is like the man who spends his life panning for gold at the edge of the river and keeps finding a few grains of gold dust. Yes, for when we seek God, we necessarily find a few tiny particles of His light, love, power and beauty. For my part, this is what I do : I work like an alchemist and never see the results of my work, but that does not discourage me because, like the man panning for gold, I rejoice in the tiny grains of gold dust that I find every day, for they are a reflection of the Philosophers' Stone, of the presence of God.

I have often told you to seek for what is unattainable, for something that you can never obtain or achieve. Yes, because, thanks to this seeking you will continually gain a little something every day. Naturally, you will never have it all, but when you concentrate on an unattainable goal, you are obliged constantly to break new ground, to move on to new regions, and it is this progress that counts. You are not asking for knowledge, kindness, health or happiness, you are asking for God, for the Absolute, and in this way you will obtain all the rest because, in order to reach God, you are obliged to pass through light, beauty, health, knowledge, wealth, love, happiness and all the other marvels that line the path that leads to God.

Blessed are those who are capable of understanding me ! Why fix your sights on some miserable little goal that will never satisfy you, that will be nothing but a disappointment when you get it ? Something that is limited can never fill the immensity of your heart and soul. Only the Absolute, God Himself, can satisfy you, and it is only if you set out in search of Him and never stop on the way that you will obtain everything, even those things that you have not asked for.

Oh, I know, this is not the first time that I have spoken to you about this ; I have been talking about it for years now. But I am obliged to repeat it, because I see you continually running after all kinds of futile things in the hope that they will fill that immense void within you. But they won't ; don't delude yourselves ! There are two paths open to you and one of them seems to lead to nothing but disillusionment whereas, in reality, it will give you everything. If you follow this path you will, one day, be able to say, 'I possess nothing and yet the whole universe belongs to me !' If you follow the other,

whatever it gives you, you will never be contented ;
you will always feel that, in spite of all you possess,
the essential has escaped you.

Anyone who understands the nature of his own
profession or activity, knows that he is bound to
meet certain difficulties and obstacles, but these are
simply the inconveniences that go with the job ; they
don't prevent him from working. Every profession
has its own drawbacks. Why do spiritualists never
know about the drawbacks inherent in their profession ? The fact that they are so easily discouraged
and ready to give up their efforts proves that they
failed to foresee the inconveniences of their trade ;
otherwise, wouldn't they continue their work with
renewed fervour ? When you are discouraged you
must know how to encourage yourselves because
of your discouragement ! I can see that you don't
understand me, and yet this is true alchemy, this
is the Philosophers' Stone.

Every day, therefore, you must get into the habit
of pulling yourself up to great heights by means of
your thought. Yes, to great heights... all the way
to the Throne of God. The fact that you see no
results does not mean that there is nothing going
on. The opacity of the matter that envelops you is
such that you cannot yet feel the slightest change ;
you see nothing, you feel nothing and so you imagine that nothing is happening. But something is
happening : at each effort you make, the path opens

up a little more, a bridge is being built between yourself and the heavenly regions and, one day, you will only need to concentrate on these regions for a few moments to feel yourself instantly flooded with joy, happiness and strength.

No spiritual practice is more important than this habit of concentrating on the image of the summit, of God. Of course, I know that Christians have never really learned to seek this sublime Being ; they prefer to pray to saints and prophets ; they are afraid to aim higher. There is nothing wrong in praying to the saints ; but it is better, far better, to get into the habit of focusing on the highest peak, on the summit. When you do this, you set certain forces in motion : an order goes out from the summit to help you and those who carry out the order can be Initiates, saints, prophets or people in your own environment ; they can even be animals or birds. Yes, animals or even nature spirits or the four Elements can be sent to carry out the orders from on high.

Some of you will say, 'But it takes too long to reach the peak ; it's too difficult ; it's not a practical proposition ! I prefer to talk to the little St Therese or St Anthony, because when I lose something he helps me to find it.' Well, I have no objection to your doing that, but you must not let that prevent you from concentrating on the summit, on the Lord Himself. Why not ? Because it is He that is in command ; everything ultimately depends on Him.

Initiatic Science explains that we are built on the same pattern as the universe : we have a summit or centre (it amounts to the same thing) within us, and this centre is our higher Self, God's representative. When you concentrate on the summit of the universe, on the Lord, when you pray to Him and implore His help, at the same time, therefore, you are making contact with the summit of your own being and setting in motion very pure, subtle vibrations which spread out and produce extremely beneficial transformations within you. Even if your prayer is not answered directly, therefore, you gain a spiritual element !

Yes, for it is quite true that your prayers are not always answered : Cosmic Intelligence sometimes judges that what you asked for would do more harm than good, so It refuses your request. But you still gain from having asked, because in doing so you have made contact with your higher Self and touched off a force, the highest force within you, which spreads out, producing sounds, perfumes and colours and influencing all your cells and all the entities that dwell in you. In this way you can gain some extremely precious elements.

The only way to obtain genuine results is to make contact with the centre, the hub of your being which organizes and orders all the rest. By way of example, suppose that you are an unknown, insignificant member of society, quite incapable of doing anything to change the destiny of your country : in order to do that, you will have to go to the centre, to the seat of government, and speak to the president or the king. In this way, by contacting the centre, you can influence the whole country. If you remain out on the fringe, you will never get anyone to obey you. So anyone who only works at the periphery will never be in a position to affect the destiny of his country, either for good or — fortunately — for ill !

You will find this same law in the inner world. As long as you fail to make contact with the centre, you may obtain a few little benefits, to be sure, but the essential will escape you. Whereas, if you are at the centre, you can turn the whole world upside down, for the centre makes you all-powerful : everything depends on you. This explains why really intelligent people don't waste their time on futile, fleeting realizations. They work without stopping, their gaze fixed on the summit, and never worry about how many years or centuries it will take to reach it. A single being can change the destiny of the world, on condition that he reaches the summit.

When you reach this summit that exists within you as a state of consciousness, you possess the same powers as the Lord Himself, and no one can stand in your way. Yes, this is the absolute truth, and by means of all that exists in the world, I can prove to you that Cosmic Intelligence has so ordered things that true strength and true power are to be found only at the summit. If you doubt this, it means that you have really not understood anything and, when one does not understand, the only thing that remains is to suffer. This is not what I hope for, for you ; on the contrary, I hope that I shall never have to see you suffer again. But when one does not understand it is impossible not to suffer. Suffering is given to human beings in order to make them understand. Actually, therefore, it is a blessing !

And now, I want to reveal to you a vital truth which all spiritual Masters have taught and which is very strongly emphasized by Initiatic Science : the fact that every human being will, one day, dwell in the region to which his thoughts are directed. When you leave this world, you will go to where your thoughts dwell. If your thoughts were habitually elevated, you will reach the most exalted regions and if, on the contrary, they were turned towards Hell, you will go to Hell. This is the greatest truth of all ! If, therefore, you ask only for intelligence, love or beauty, you can be absolutely sure that no force in nature will ever be able to prevent you from dwelling in the region of your choice, the region in which your thoughts and desires have always dwelt.

By the same author

Izvor Collection
TABLE OF CONTENTS

205 – SEXUAL FORCE OR THE WINGED DRAGON

1. The Winged Dragon – 2. Love and Sexuality – 3. The Sexual Force is Essential for Life on Earth – 4. Pleasure : I – Do not Seek Pleasure for it Will Impoverish You – II – Replace Pleasure with Work – 5. The Dangers of Tantric Yoga – 6. Love without Waiting to be Loved – 7. Love is Everywhere in the Universe – 8. Spiritual Love is a Higher Way of Feeding Ourselves – 9. A High Ideal Transforms Sexual Energy – 10. Open Your Love to a Higher Path.

206 – A PHILOSOPHY OF UNIVERSALITY

1. What is a Sect ? – 2. No Church is Eternal – 3. The Spirit Behind the Form – 4. The Advent of the Church of St. John – 5. The Foundations of a Universal Religion – 6. The Great Universal White Brotherhood – 7. For a Universal Notion of the Family – 8. Brotherhood, a Higher State of Consciousness – 9. The Annual Conventions at the Bonfin – 10. The Universal Dimension of All Our Activities.

207 – WHAT IS A SPIRITUAL MASTER ?

1. How to Recognize a True Spiritual Master – 2. The Necessity for a Spiritual Master – 3. The Sorcerer's Apprentice – 4. The Exotic Should not be Confused with Spirituality – 5. Learn How to Balance the Material and Spiritual Worlds – 6. A Master is a Mirror Reflecting the Truth – 7. A Master is There Only to Give Light – 8. The Disciple and His Master – 9. The Universal Dimension of a Master – 10. The Magical Presence of a Master – 11. Identification – 12. 'Except Ye Become as Little Children...'

208 – THE EGREGOR OF THE DOVE
OR THE REIGN OF PEACE

1. Towards a Better Understanding of Peace – 2. The Advantages of Unity amongst Nations – 3. Aristocracy and Democracy – 4. About Money – 5. The Distribution of Wealth – 6. Communism and Capitalism – 7. Towards a New Understanding of Economics – 8. What Every Politician Should Know – 9. The Kingdom of God.

Self — 8. The Silent Voice of the Higher Self — 9. Only by Serving the Divine Nature — 10. Address the Higher Self in Others — 11. Man's Return to God, the Victory.

214 — HOPE FOR THE WORLD: SPIRITUAL GALVANOPLASTY

1. What is Spiritual Galvanoplasty ? — 2. Reflections of the Two Principles — 3. Marriages Made in Heaven — 4. Love Freely Given — 5. Love on the Lower Plane — 6. Love on the Higher Plane — 7. Love's Goal is Light — 8. The Solar Nature of Sexual Energy — 9. Mankind Transformed — 10. The Original Experiment and the New One — 11. Replenish the Earth ! — 12. Woman's place — 13. The Cosmic Child.

215 — THE TRUE MEANING OF CHRIST'S TEACHING

1. 'Our Father Which Art in Heaven' — 2. 'My Father and I Are One' — 3. 'Be Ye Perfect, Even as Your Father Who is in Heaven is Perfect' — 4. 'Seek Ye First the Kingdom of God and His Justice' — 5. 'On Earth as it is in Heaven' — 6. 'He That Eateth My Flesh and Drinketh My Blood Hath Eternal Life' — 7. 'Father, Forgive Them, For They Know Not What They Do' — 8. 'Unto Him that Smiteth Thee on the One Cheek...' — 9. 'Watch and Pray'.

216 — THE LIVING BOOK OF NATURE

1. The Living Book of Nature — 2. Day and Night — 3. Spring Water or Stagnant Water — 4. Marriage, a Universal Symbol — 5. Distilling the Quintessence — 6. The Power of Fire — 7. The Naked Truth — 8. Building a House — 9. Red and White — 10. The River of Life — 11. The New Jerusalem — Perfect Man. I — The Gates. II — The Foundations — 12. Learning to Read and Write.

217 — NEW LIGHT ON THE GOSPELS

1. 'Men do not Put New Wine into Old Bottles' — 2. 'Except Ye Become as Little Children' — 3. The Unjust Stewart — 4. 'Lay up for Yourselves Treasures in Heaven' — 5. The Strait Gate — 6. 'Let Him Which is on the Housetop not Come

222 – MAN'S PSYCHIC LIFE: ELEMENTS AND STRUCTURES

1. Know Thyself – 2. The Synoptic Table – 3. Several Souls and Several Bodies – 4. Heart, Mind, Soul and Spirit – 5. The Apprenticeship of the Will – 6. Body, Soul and Spirit – 7. Outer Knowledge and Inner Knowledge – 8. From Intellect to Intelligence – 9. True Illumination – 10. The Causal Body – 11. Consciousness – 12. The Subconscious – 13. The Higher Self.

223 – CREATION: ARTISTIC AND SPIRITUAL

1. Art, Science and Religion – 2. The Divine Sources of Inspiration – 3. The Work of the Imagination – 4. Prose and Poetry – 5. The Human Voice – 6. Choral Singing – 7. How to Listen to Music – 8. The Magic Power of a Gesture – 9. Beauty – 10. Idealization as a Means of Creation – 11. A Living Masterpiece – 12. Building the Temple – Postface.

224 – THE POWERS OF THOUGHT

1. The Reality of Spiritual Work – 2. Thinking the Future – 3. Psychic Pollution – 4. Thoughts are Living Beings – 5. How Thought Produces Material Results – 6. Striking a Balance between Matter and Spirit – 7. The Strength of the Spirit – 8. Rules for Spiritual Work – 9. Thoughts as Weapons – 10. The Power of Concentration – 11. Meditation – 12. Creative Prayer – 13. Reaching for the Unattainable.

Editor-Distributor

Editions PROSVETA S.A. – B.P. 12 – 83601 Fréjus Cedex (France)

Distributors

AUSTRIA
MANDALA
Verlagsauslieferung für Esoterik
A-6094 Axams, Innsbruckstraße 7

BELGIUM
PROSVETA BENELUX
Van Putlei 105 B-2548 Lint

N.V. MAKLU Somersstraat 13-15
B-2000 Antwerpen

VANDER S.A.
Av. des Volontaires 321
B-1150 Bruxelles

BRITISH ISLES
PROSVETA Ldt
The Doves Nest
Duddleswell Uckfield,
East Sussex TN 22 3JJ

Trade orders to :
ELEMENT Books Ltd
Unit 25 Longmead Shaftesbury
Dorset SP7 8PL

CANADA
PROSVETA Inc.
1565 Montée Masson
Duvernay est, Laval, Que. H7E 4P2

GERMANY
URANIA – Rudolf-Diesel-Ring 26
D-8029 Sauerlach

HOLLAND
STICHTING
PROSVETA NEDERLAND
Zeestraat 50
2042 LC Zandvoort

HONG KONG
HELIOS
J. Ryan
P.O. BOX 8503
General Post Office, Hong Kong

IRELAND
PROSVETA IRL.
84 Irishtown – Clonmel

ITALY
PROSVETA Coop. a.r.l.
Cas. post. 13046 – 20130 Milano

LUXEMBOURG
PROSVETA BENELUX
Van Putlei 105 B-2548 Lint

NORWAY
PROSVETA NORGE
Postboks 5101
1501 Moss

PORTUGAL
PUBLICAÇÕES
EUROPA-AMERICA Ltd
Est Lisboa-Sintra KM 14
2726 Mem Martins Codex

SPAIN
ASOCIACIÓN PROSVETA
Caspe 41
E-08010 Barcelona

SWITZERLAND
PROSVETA
Société Coopérative
CH - 1808 Les Monts-de-Corsier

UNITED STATES
PROSVETA U.S.A.
P.O. Box 49614
Los Angeles, California 90049

PRINTED IN FRANCE
APRIL 1988
EDITIONS PROSVETA
Z.I. DU CAPITOU – B.P.12
83601 FRÉJUS CEDEX
FRANCE

– N° d'impression : 1590 –
Dépôt légal : Avril 1988
Printed in France